FOR ORGANS, PIANOS & ELECTRONIC KEYBOARDS

E-Z PLAY TODAY

245

THE BEST OF

Simon & Garfunkel

ISBN 978-0-7935-7950-1

HAL•LEONARD®
CORPORATION
7777 W. BLUEMOUND RD. P.O. BOX 13819 MILWAUKEE, WI 53213

Visit Hal Leonard Online at
www.halleonard.com

THE BEST OF
SIMON & GARFUNKEL

SIMON & GARFUNKEL HITS

PAUL SIMON HITS

America

Registration 6
Rhythm: Waltz

Words and Music by
Paul Simon

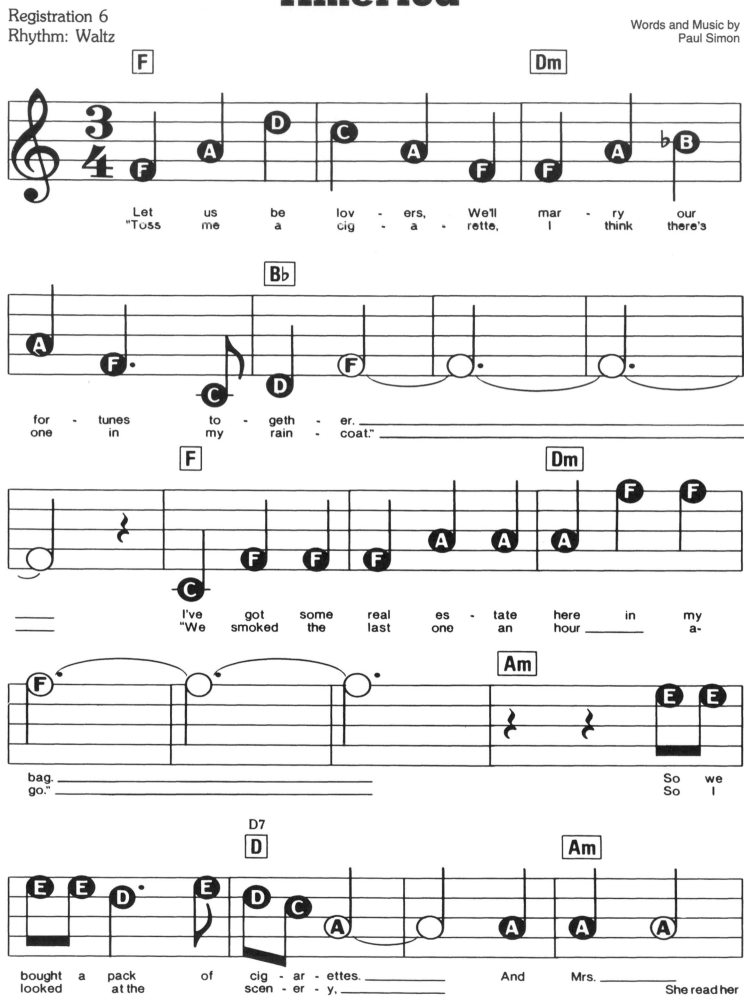

Wag - ner's pies. _____ And walked
magazine; _____ And the moon

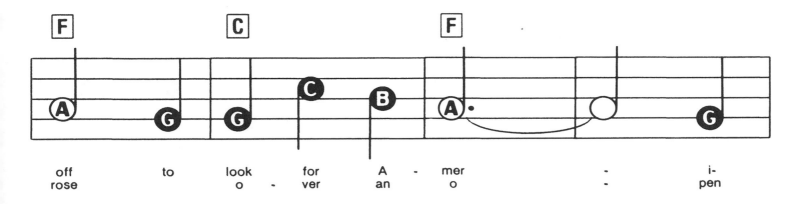

off to look for A - mer - i-
rose o - ver an o - pen

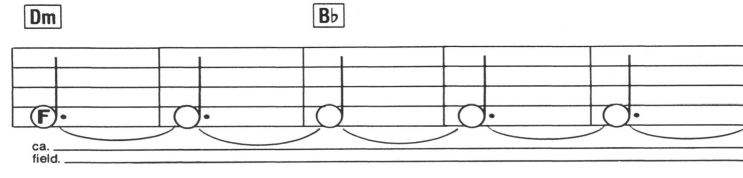

ca. _____
field. _____

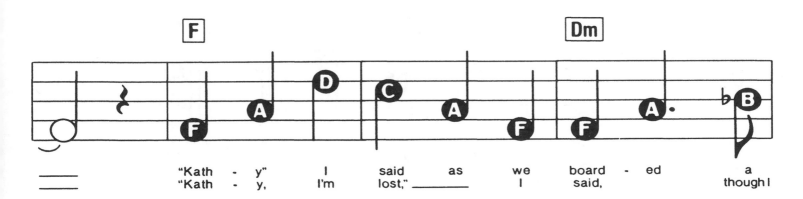

"Kath - y" I said as we board - ed a
"Kath - y, I'm lost," _____ I said, though I

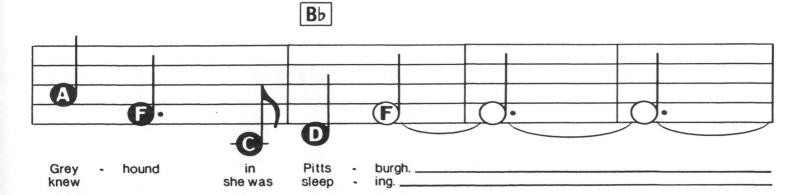

Grey - hound in Pitts - burgh. _____
knew she was sleep - ing. _____

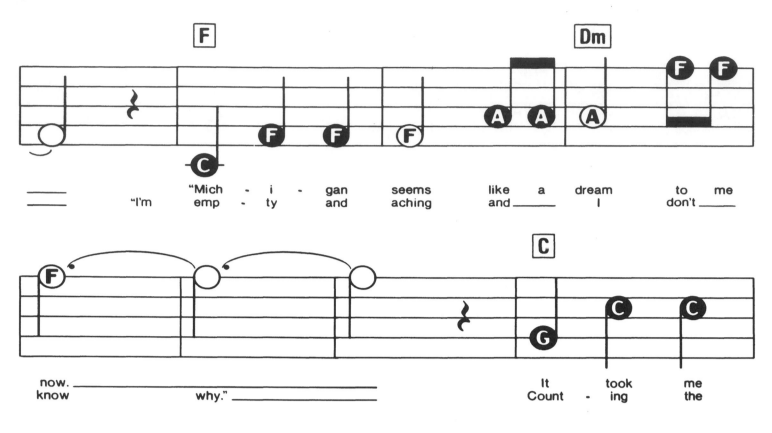

"Mich - i - gan seems like a dream to me
"I'm emp - ty and aching and _____ I don't _____

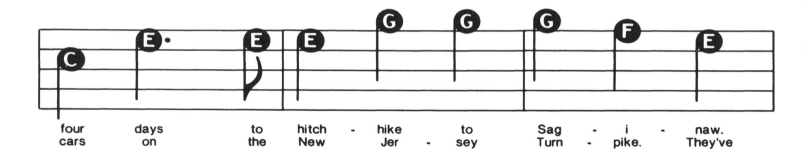

now. _____
know why." _____

It took me
Count - ing me the

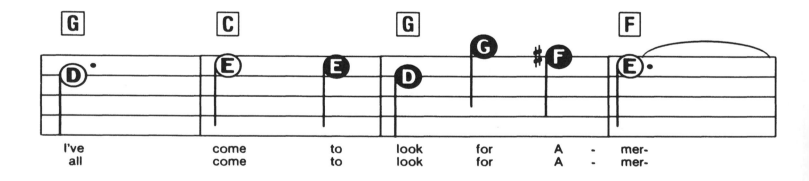

four days to hitch - hike to Sag - i - naw.
cars on the New Jer - sey Turn - pike. They've

I've all come to look for A - mer-
all come to look for A - mer-

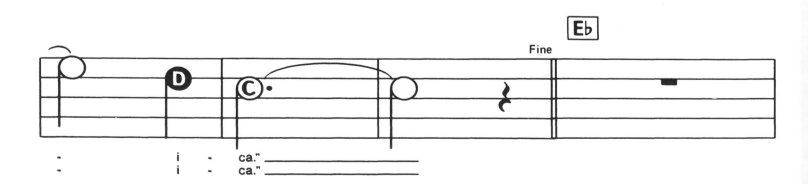

Fine

- i - ca." _____
- i - ca." _____

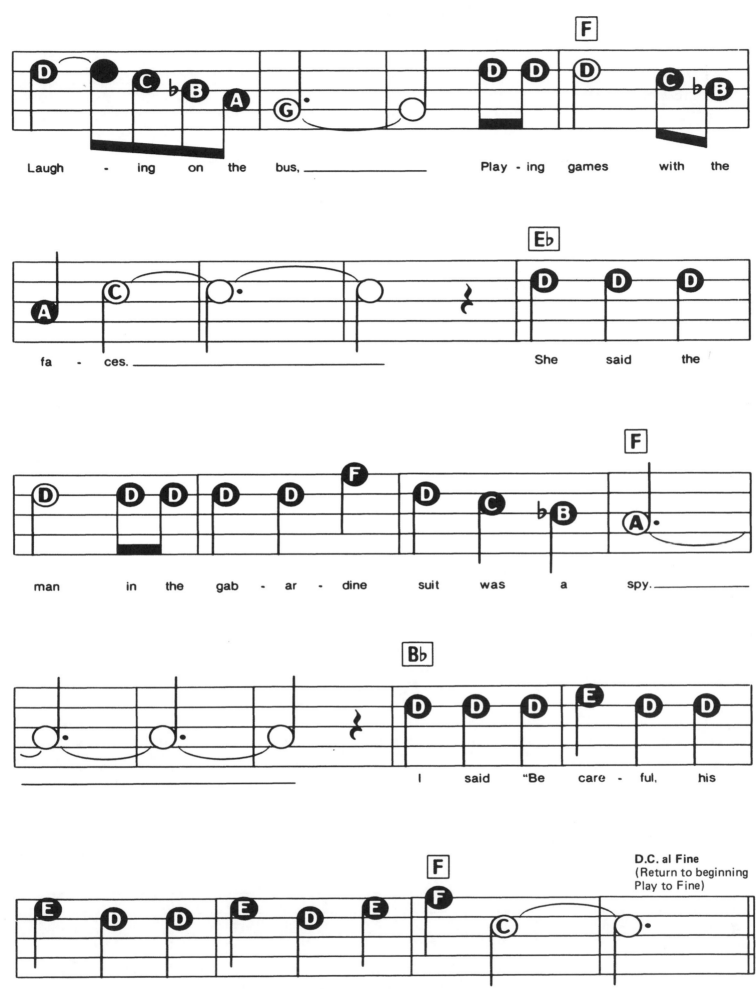

The Boxer

Registration 8
Rhythm: Swing

Words and Music by
Paul Simon

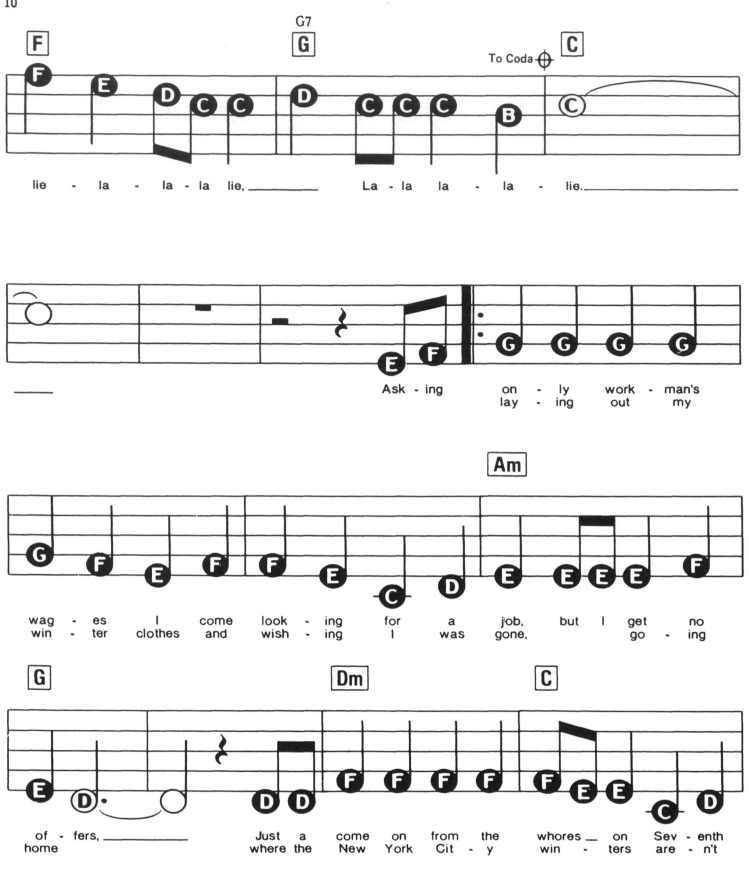

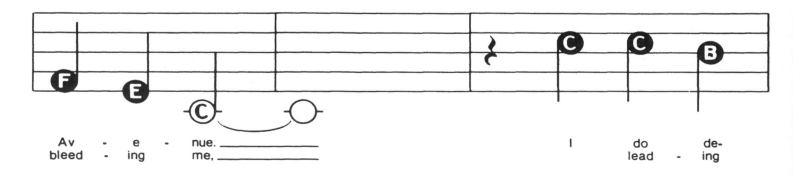

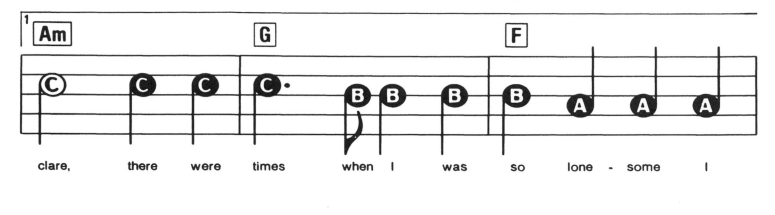

clare, there were times when I was so lone - some I

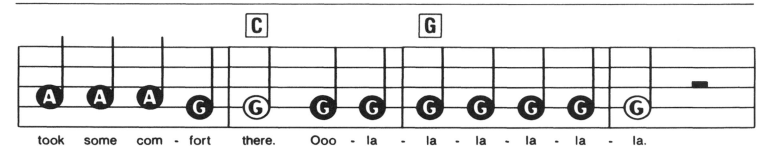

took some com - fort there. Ooo - la - la - la - la - la - la.

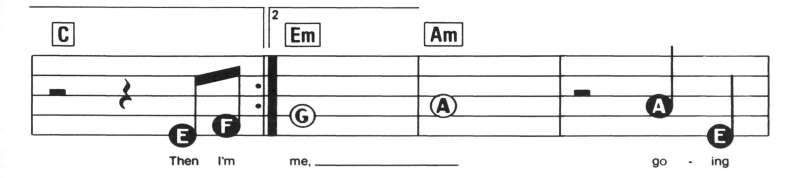

Then I'm me, _____ go - ing

D.C. al Coda
(Return to beginning
Play to ⊕ and skip
to Coda)

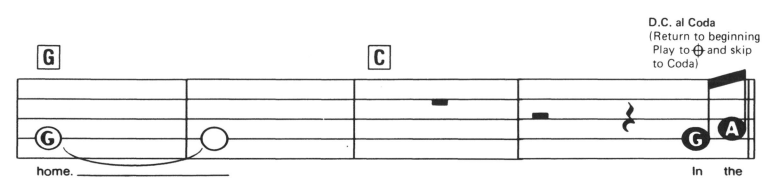

home. _____ In the

⊕ CODA

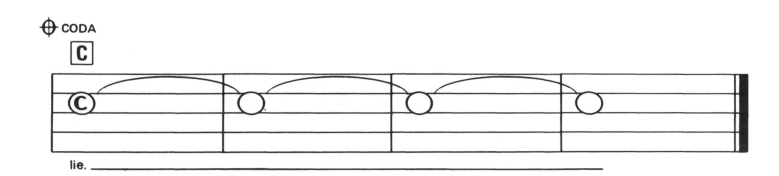

lie. _____

Bridge Over Troubled Water

Registration 3
Rhythm: Slow Rock or Ballad

Words and Music by
Paul Simon

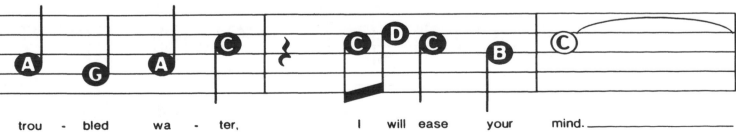

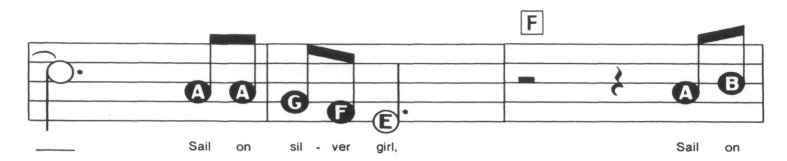

Sail on sil - ver girl,   Sail on

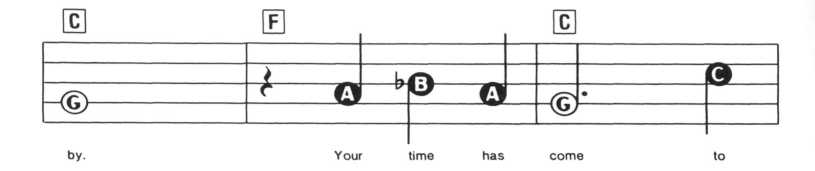

by.   Your time has come to

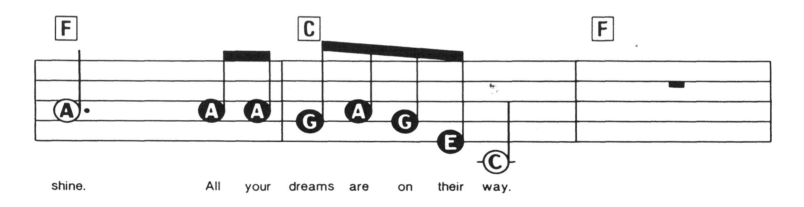

shine.   All your dreams are on their way.

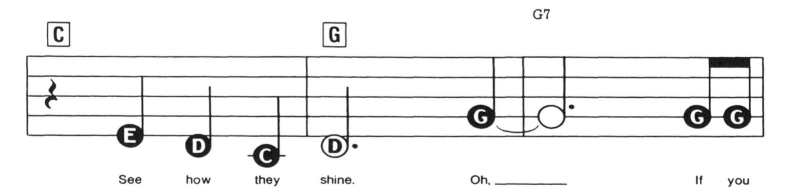

See how they shine.   Oh, _____   If you

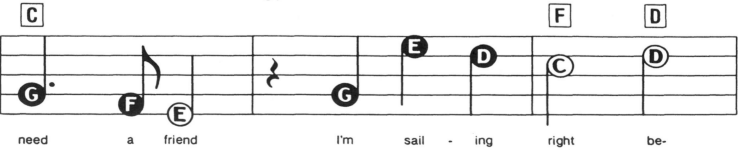

need a friend   I'm sail - ing right be-

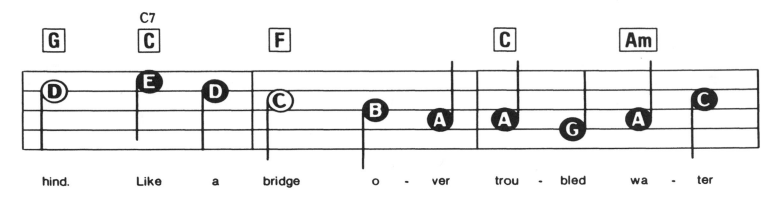

hind.   Like a bridge o - ver trou - bled wa - ter

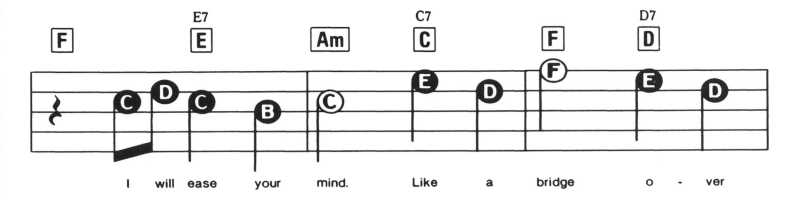

I will ease your mind.   Like a bridge o - ver

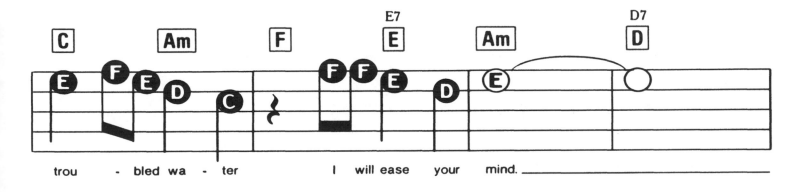

trou - bled wa - ter   I will ease your mind.

Cecilia

Registration 9
Rhythm: March

Words and Music by
Paul Simon

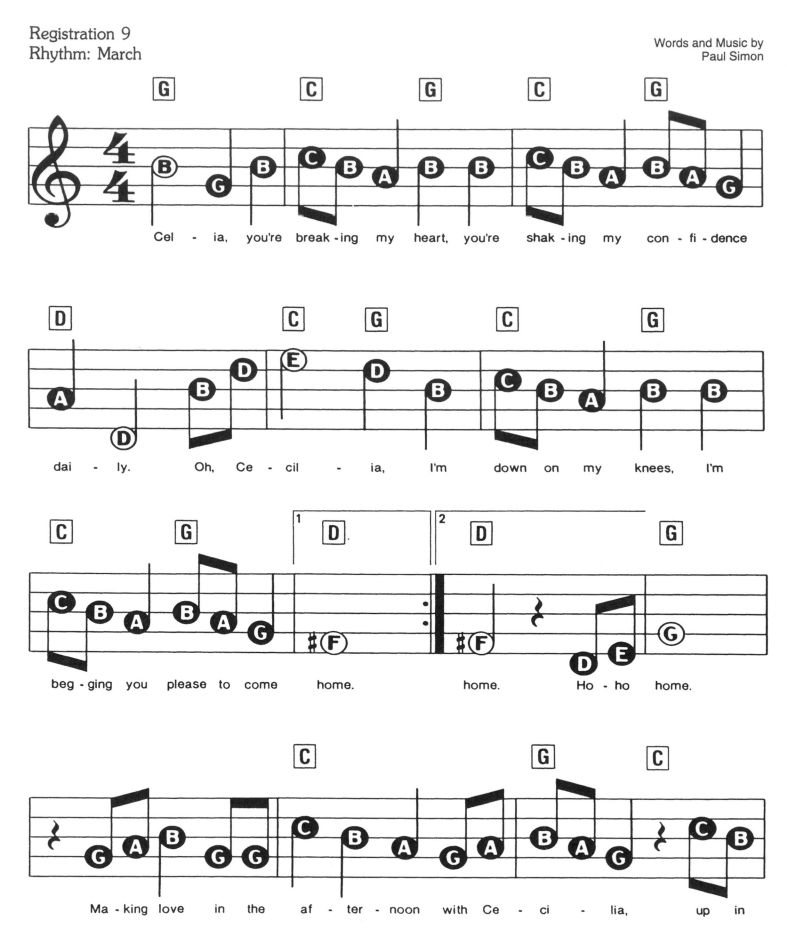

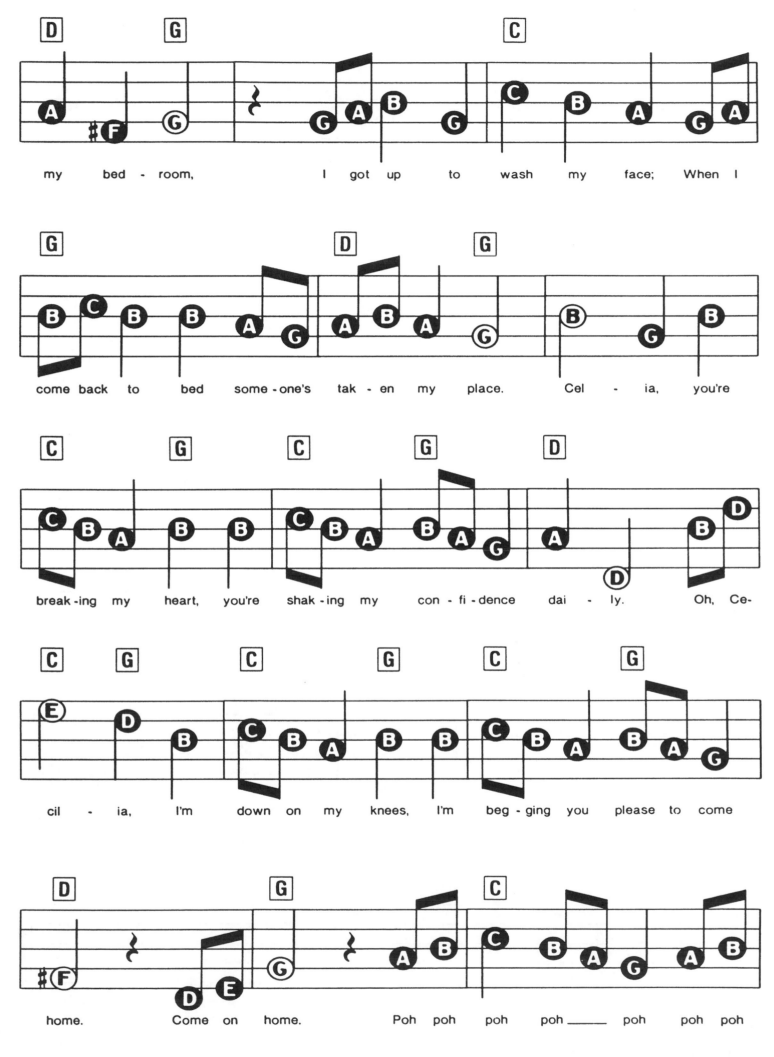

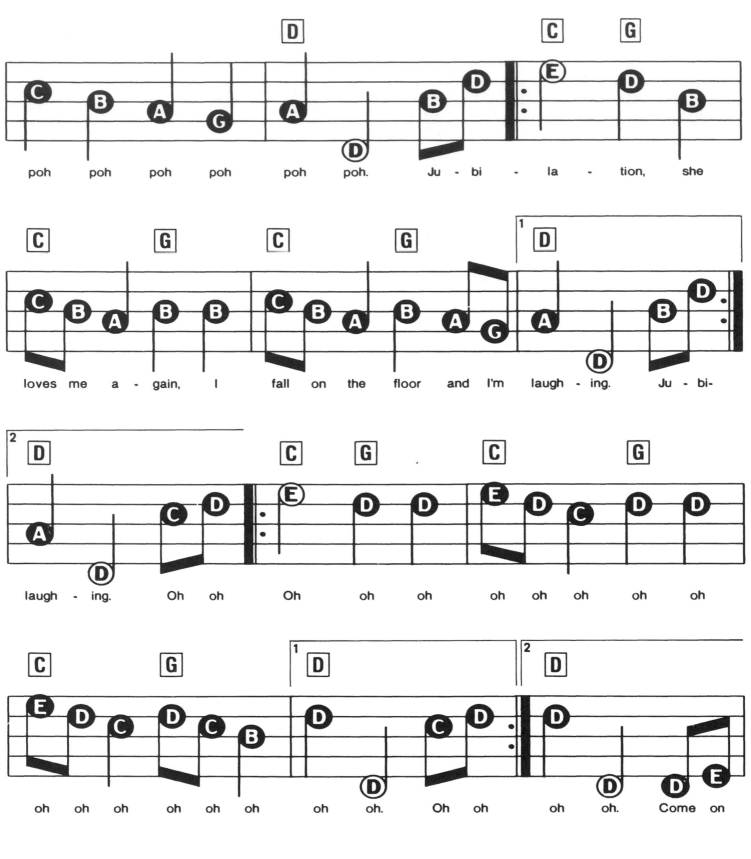

El Condor Pasa
(If I Could)

Registration 9
Rhythm: Rock

English Lyric by Paul Simon
Musical Arrangement Written by Jorge Milchberg and Daniel Robles

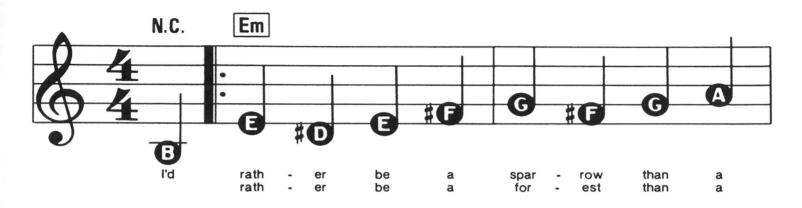

I'd
rath - er be a spar - row than a
rath - er be a for - est than a

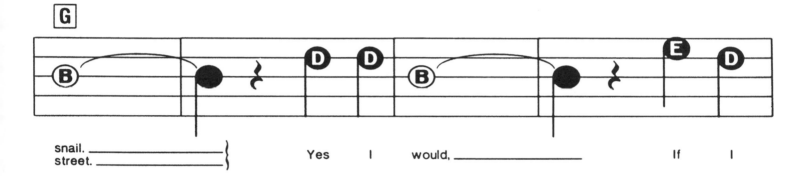

snail. _____
street. _____
Yes I would, _____
If I

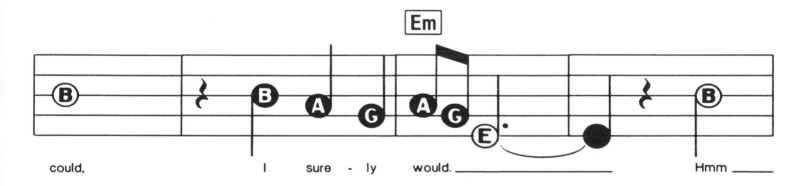

could,
I sure - ly would. _____
Hmm ____

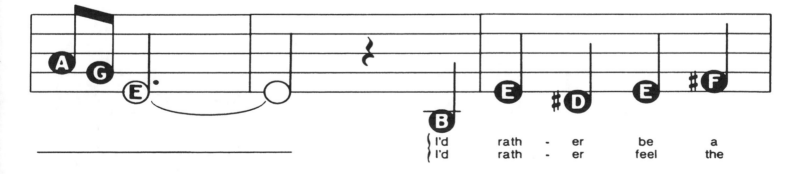

I'd rath - er be a
I'd rath - er feel the

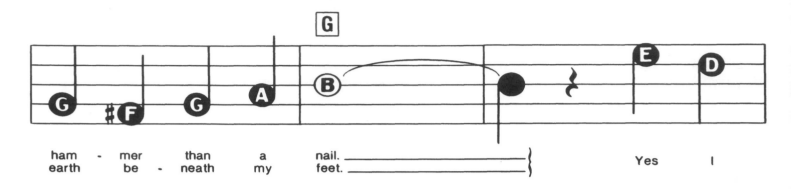

ham - mer than a nail. _____ } Yes I
earth be - neath my feet. _____

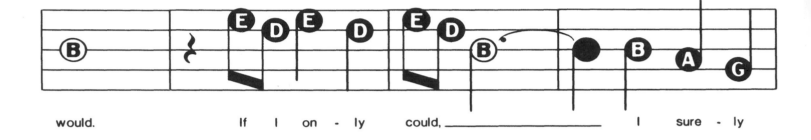

would.   If I on - ly could, _____ I sure - ly

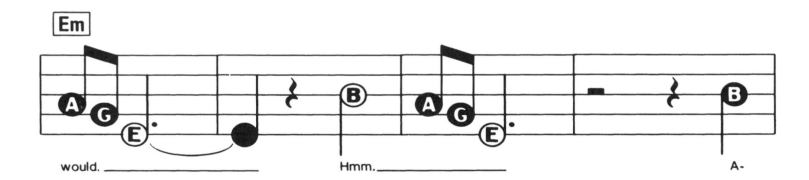

would. _____   Hmm. _____   A-

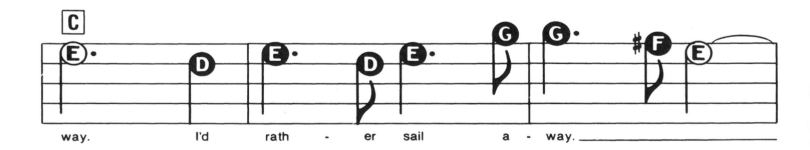

way.   I'd rath - er sail a - way. _____

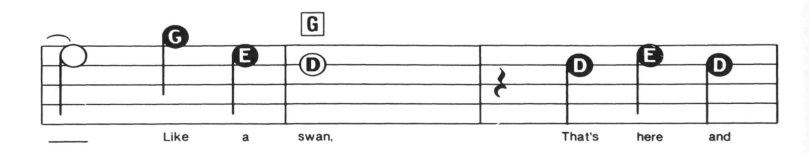

___ Like a swan,   That's here and

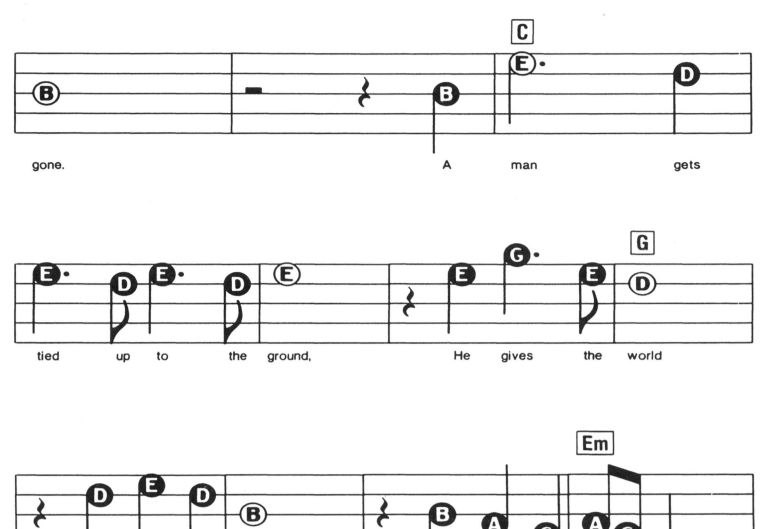

gone.   A   man   gets

tied   up   to   the   ground,   He   gives   the   world

its   sad - dest   sound,   Its   sad - dest   sound._____

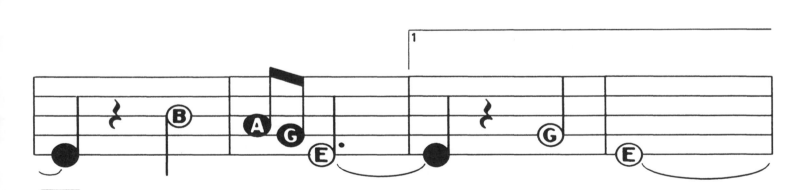

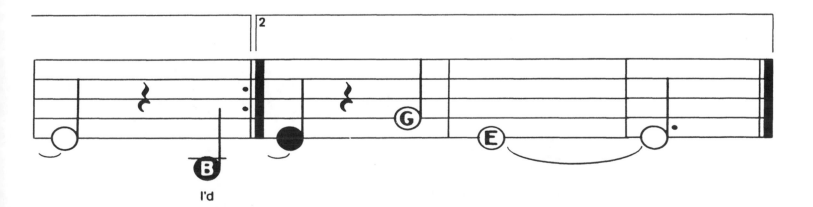

I'd

The 59th Street Bridge Song
(Feelin' Groovy)

Registration 8
Rhythm: Rock

Words and Music by
Paul Simon

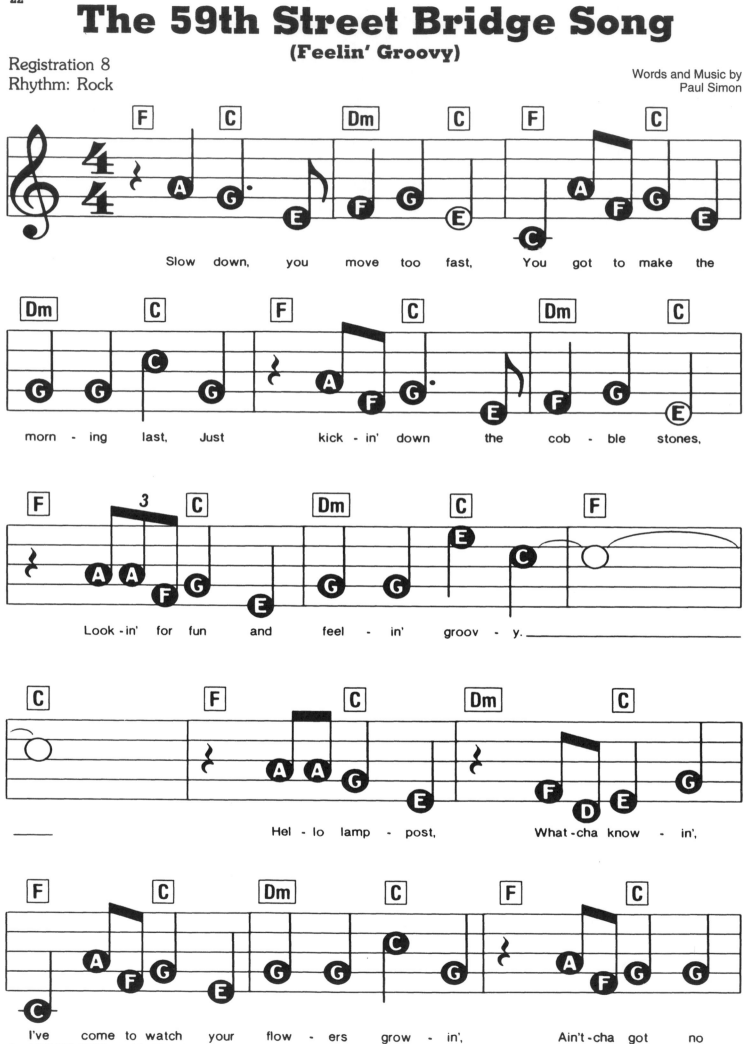

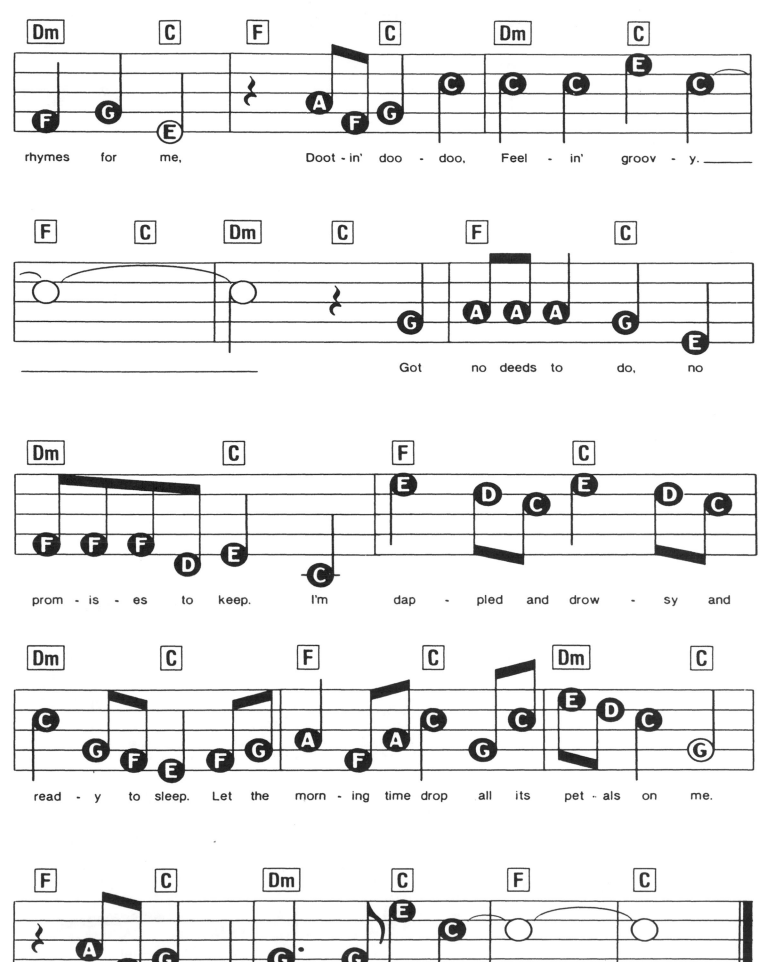

Fifty Ways to Leave Your Lover

Registration 7
Rhythm: Rock or Disco

Words and Music by
Paul Simon

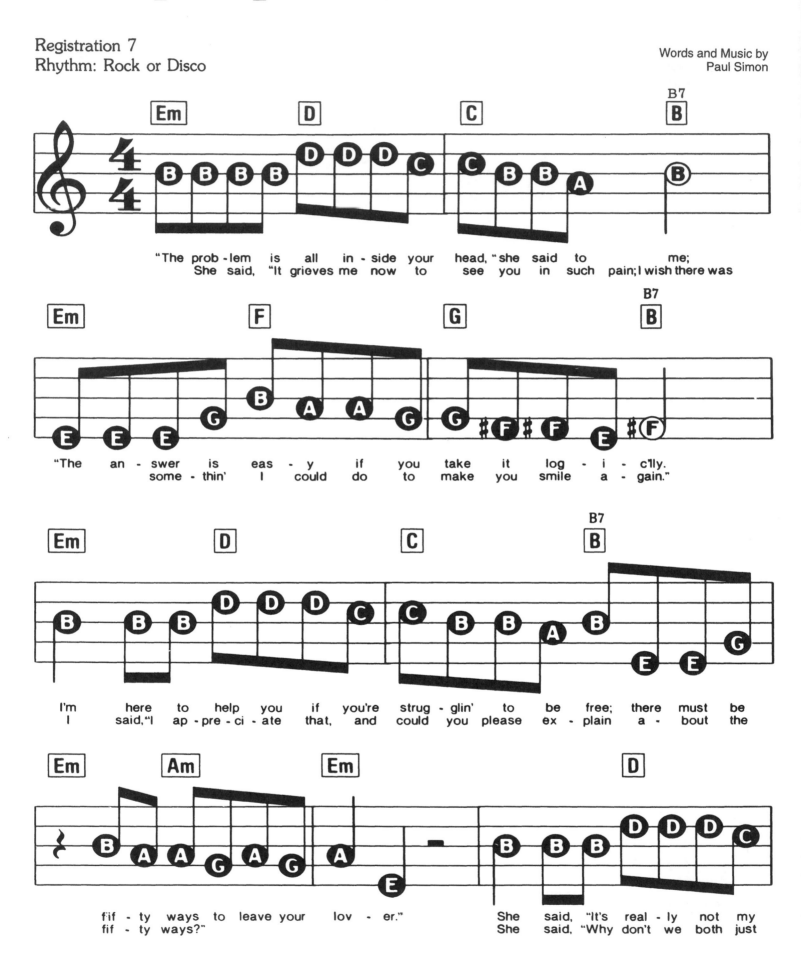

"The prob - lem is all in - side your head, "she said to me;
She said, "It grieves me now to see you in such pain; I wish there was

"The an - swer is eas - y if you take it log - i - c'lly.
some - thin' I could do to make you smile a - gain."

I'm here to help you if you're strug - glin' to be free; there must be
I said, "I ap - pre - ci - ate that, and could you please ex - plain a - bout the

fif - ty ways to leave your lov - er."
fif - ty ways?"

She said, "It's real - ly not my
She said, "Why don't we both just

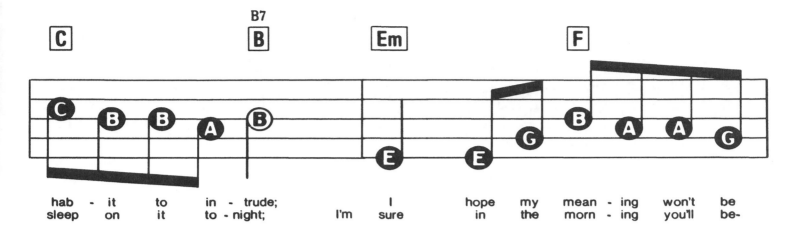

hab - it to in - trude;   I   hope my mean - ing won't be
sleep on it to - night; I'm sure in the morn - ing you'll be-

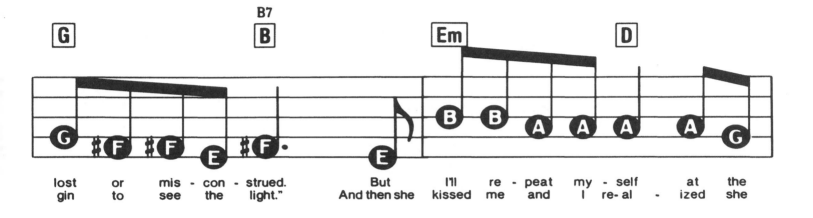

lost or mis - con - strued. But I'll re - peat my - self at the
gin to see the light." And then she kissed me and I re - al - ized she

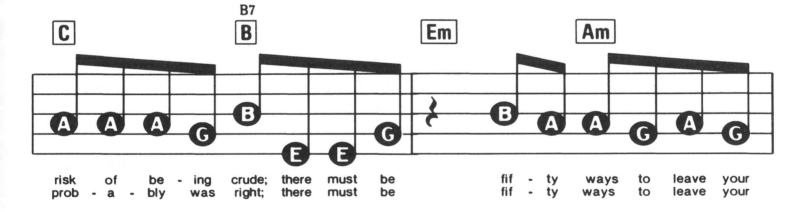

risk of be - ing crude; there must be   fif - ty ways to leave your
prob - a - bly was right; there must be   fif - ty ways to leave your

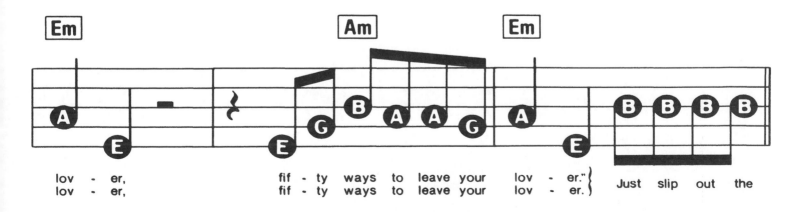

lov - er,   fif - ty ways to leave your lov - er." Just slip out the
lov - er,   fif - ty ways to leave your lov - er.

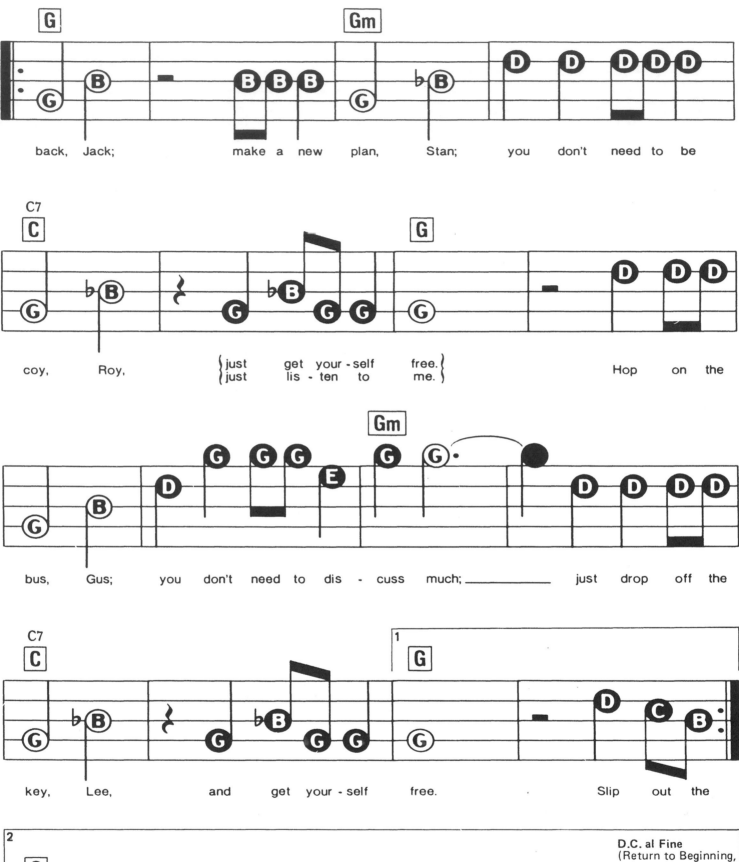

back, Jack;   make a new plan, Stan;   you don't need to be

coy, Roy,   just get your-self free.   Hop on the
                  just lis-ten to me.

bus, Gus;   you don't need to dis-cuss much; _____ just drop off the

key, Lee,   and get your-self free.   Slip out the

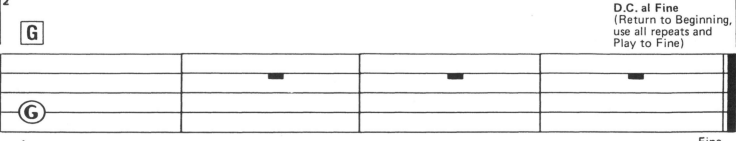

D.C. al Fine
(Return to Beginning,
use all repeats and
Play to Fine)

free.   Fine

Homeward Bound

Registration 8
Rhythm: Swing

Words and Music by
Paul Simon

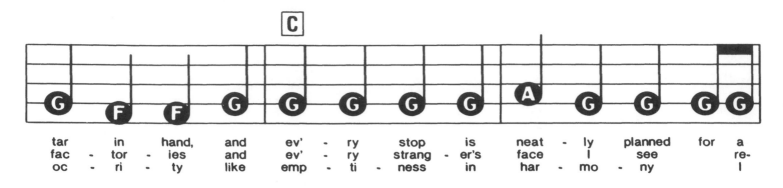

tar in hand, and ev' - ry stop is neat - ly planned for a
fac - tor - ies and ev' - ry strang - er's face I see re-
oc - ri - ty like emp - ti - ness in har - mo - ny I

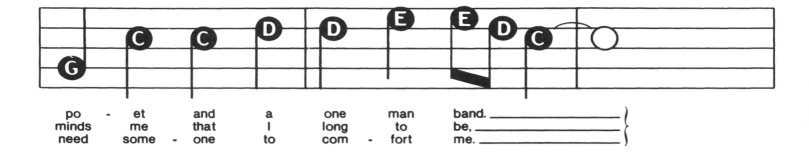

po - et and a one man band. _____
minds me that I long to be, _____
need some - one to com - fort me. _____

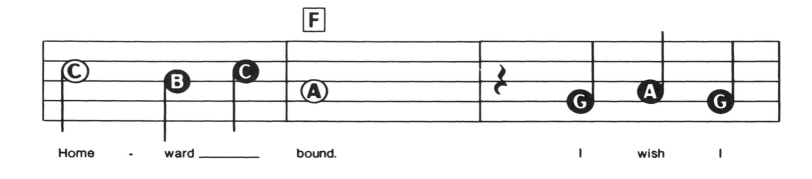

Home - ward _____ bound. I wish I

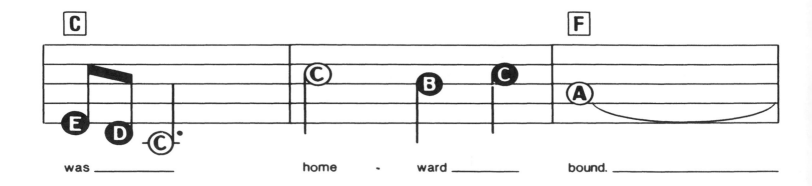

was _____ home - ward _____ bound. _____

29

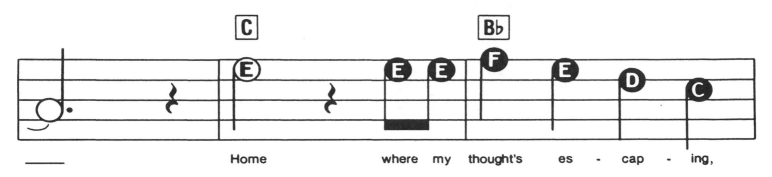

Home where my thought's es - cap - ing,

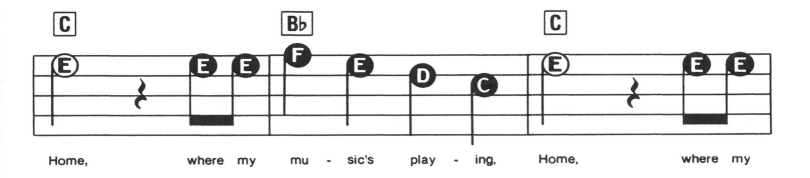

Home, where my mu - sic's play - ing, Home, where my

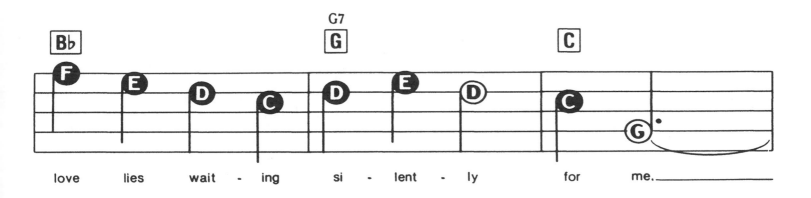

love lies wait - ing si - lent - ly for me._____

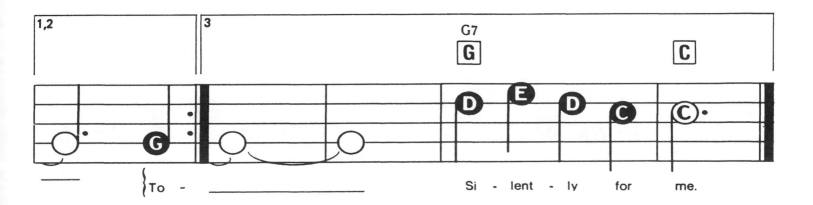

_____ {To - _____ Si - lent - ly for me.

I Am a Rock

Registration 5
Rhythm: Rock

Words and Music by
Paul Simon

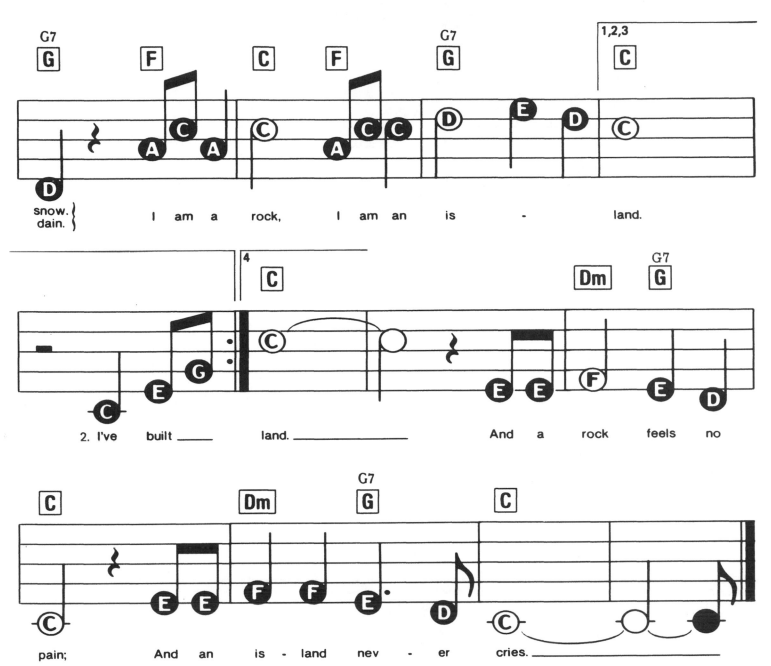

ADDITIONAL VERSES

3. Don't talk of love;
But I've heard the word before;
It's sleeping in my memory.
I won't disturb the slumber
Of feelings that have died.
If I never loved I never would have cried.
I am a rock, I am an island.

4. I have my books
And my poetry to protect me;
I am shielded in my armour,
Hiding in my room,
Safe within my womb.
I touch no one and no one touches me.
I am a rock, I am an island.
(To 4th ending)

Kodachrome

Registration 6
Rhythm: Slow Rock or Ballad

Words and Music by
Paul Simon

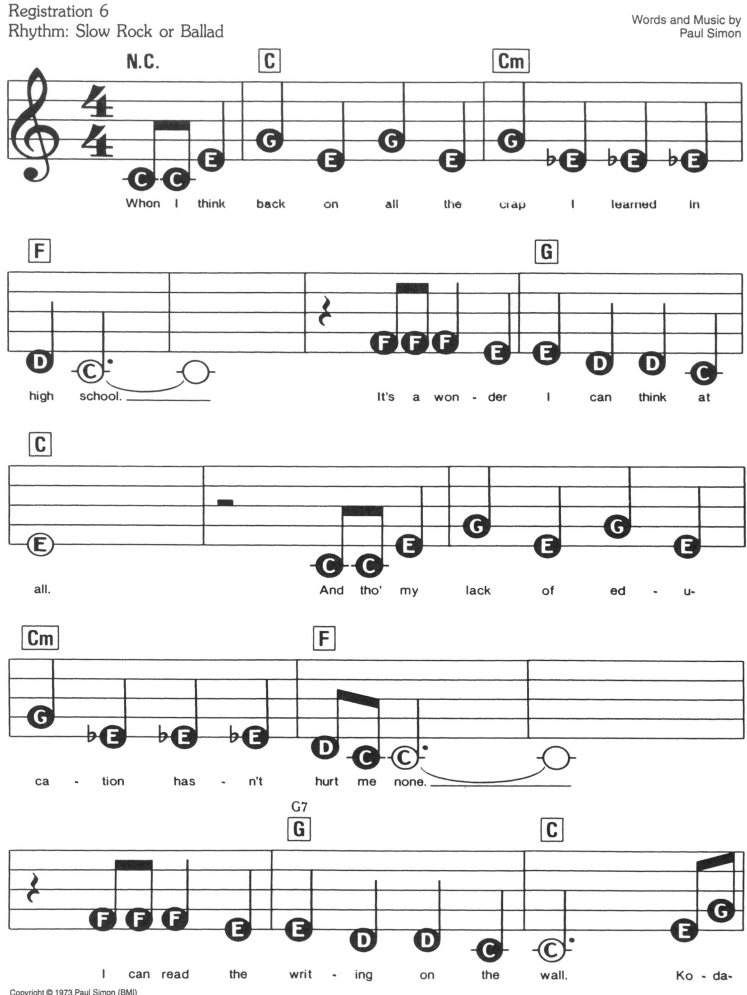

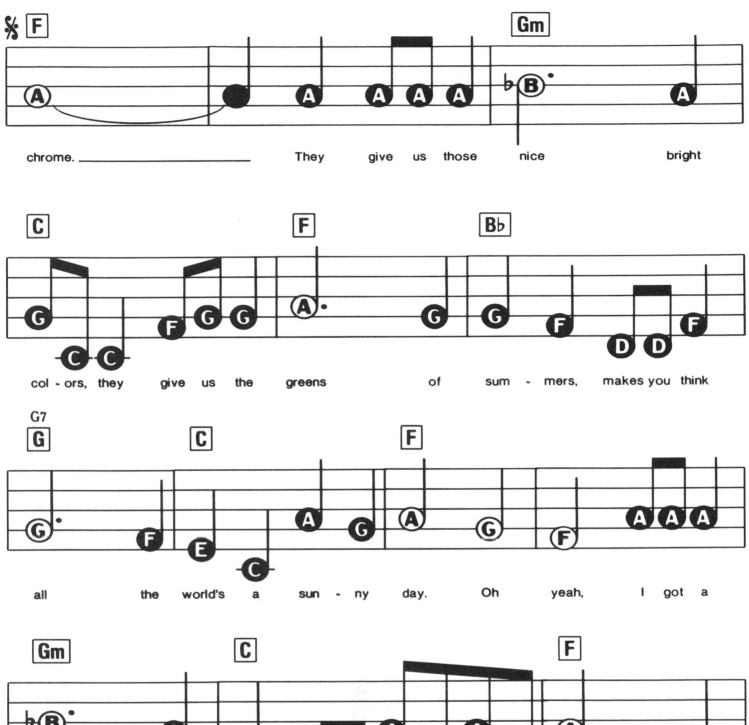

chrome. _____ They give us those nice bright

col - ors, they give us the greens of sum - mers, makes you think

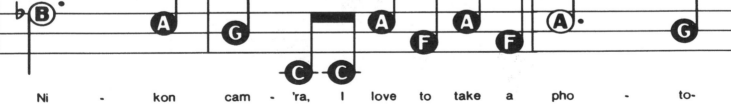

all the world's a sun - ny day. Oh yeah, I got a

Ni - kon cam - 'ra, I love to take a pho - to-

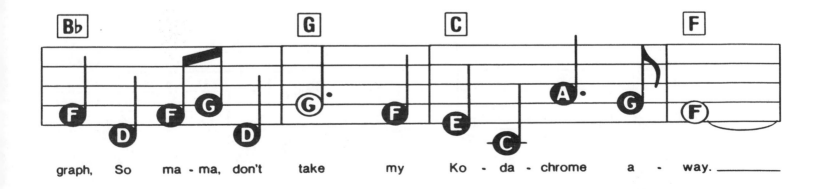

graph, So ma - ma, don't take my Ko - da - chrome a - way. _____

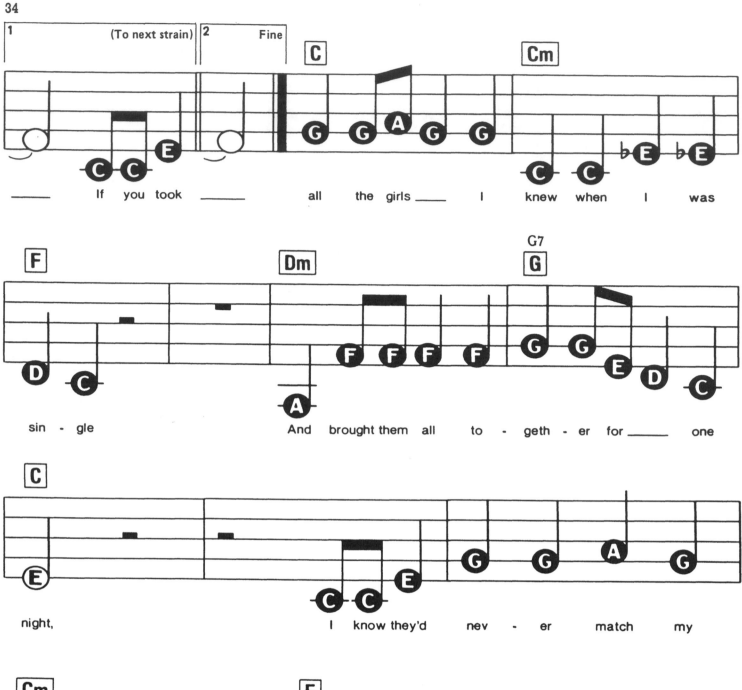

If you took _____ all the girls _____ I knew when I was single

And brought them all to - geth - er for _____ one night,

I know they'd nev - er match my sweet im - ag - i - na - tion, _____

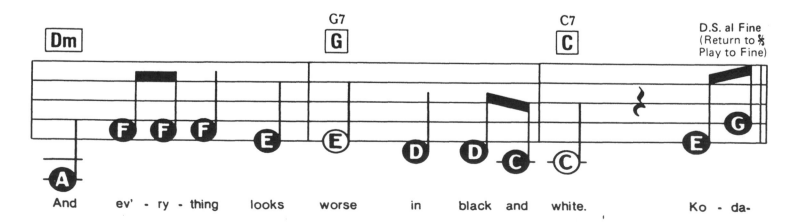

And ev' - ry - thing looks worse in black and white. Ko - da-

Mother and Child Reunion

Registration 2
Rhythm: Rock or Pop

Words and Music by
Paul Simon

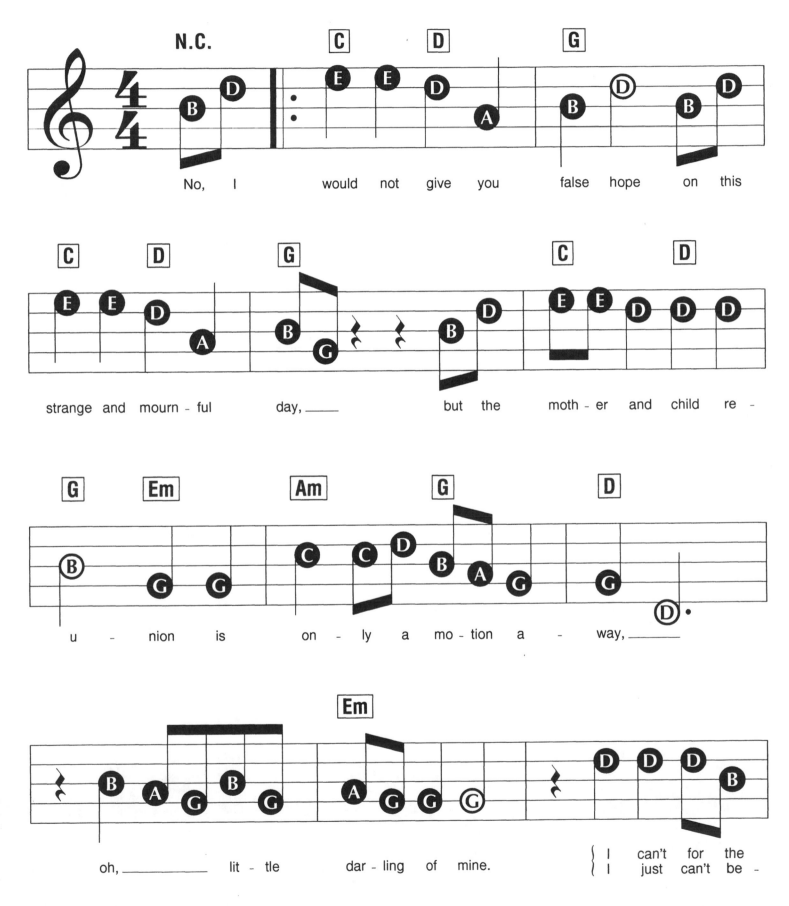

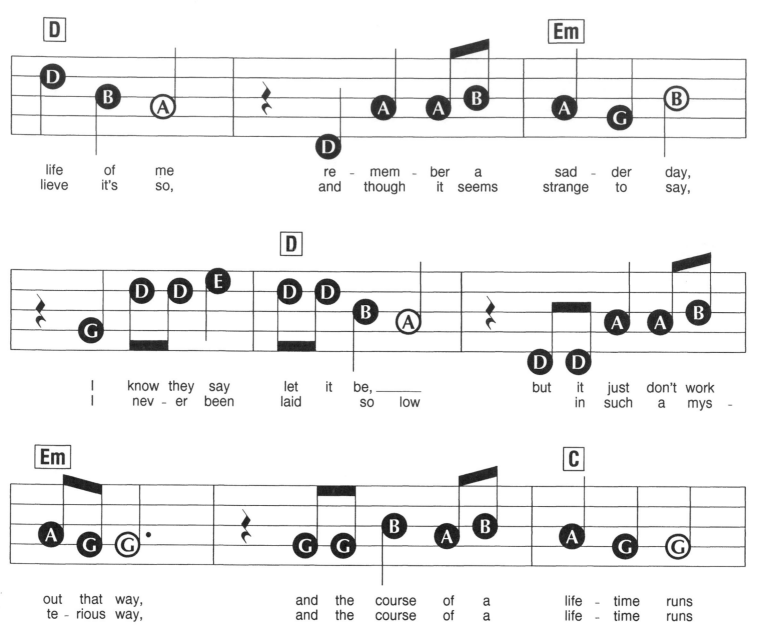

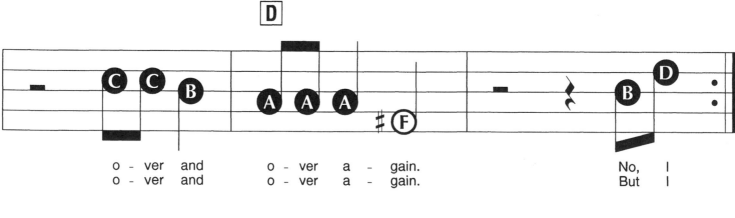

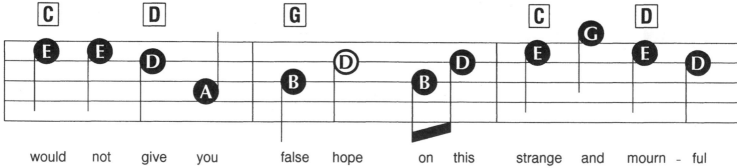

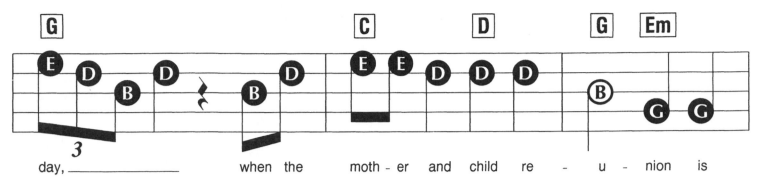

day, _____ when the moth - er and child re - u - nion is

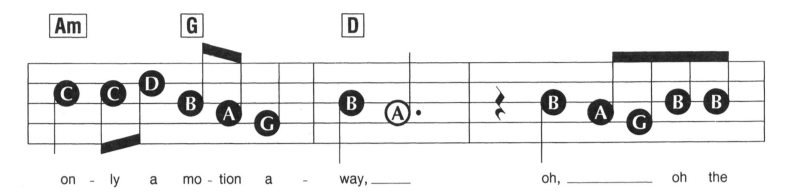

on - ly a mo - tion a - way, _____ oh, _____ oh the

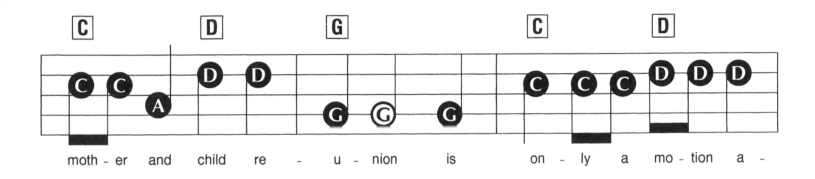

moth - er and child re - u - nion is on - ly a mo - tion a -

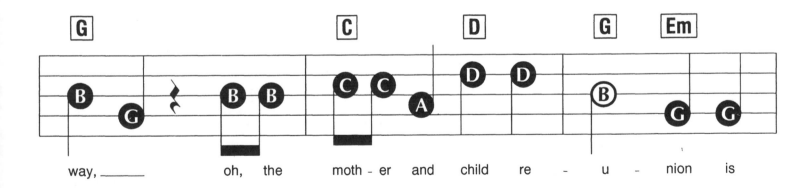

way, _____ oh, the moth - er and child re - u - nion is

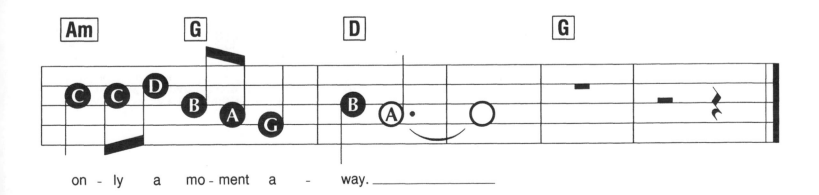

on - ly a mo - ment a - way. _____

Loves Me Like a Rock

Registration 2
Rhythm: Rock

Words and Music by
Paul Simon

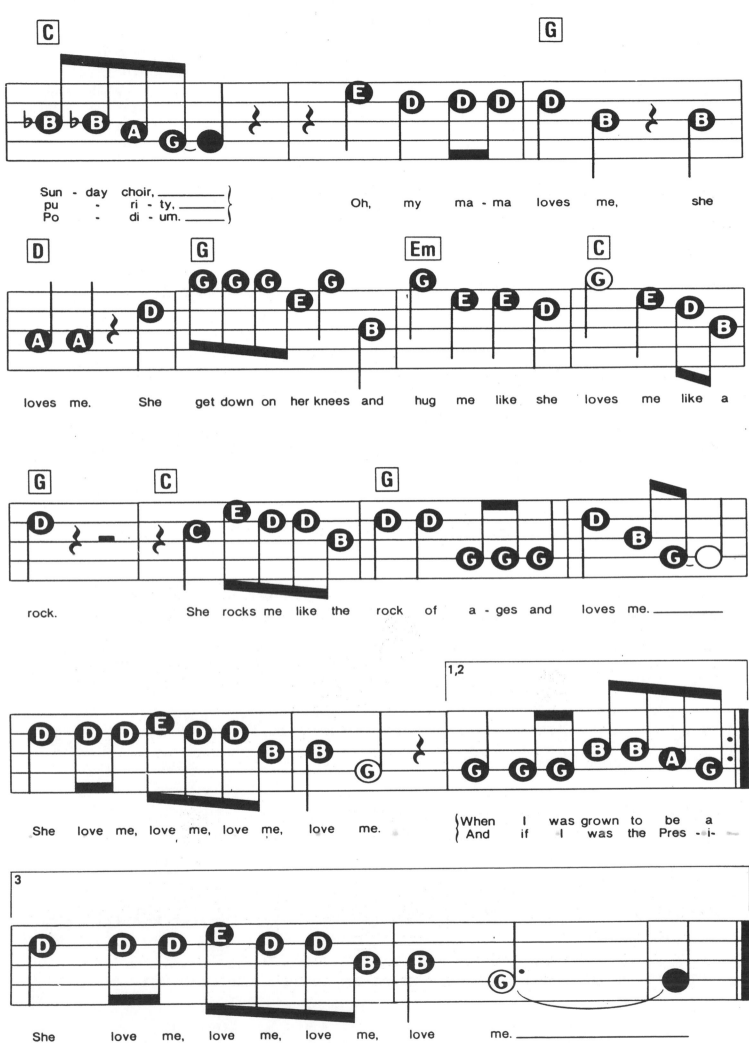

Me and Julio Down by the School Yard

Registration 9
Rhythm: Samba or Latin

Words and Music by
Paul Simon

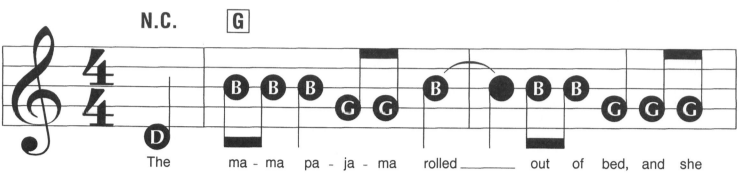

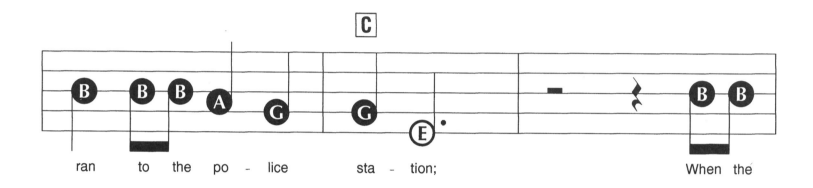

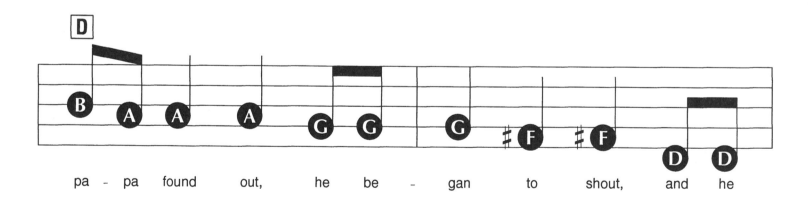

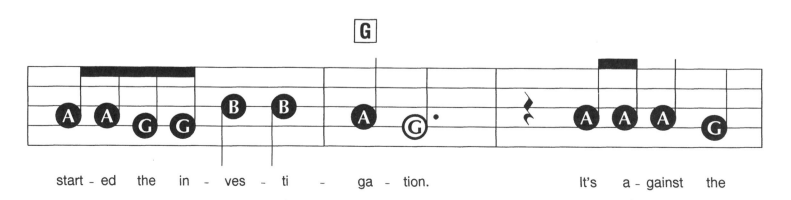

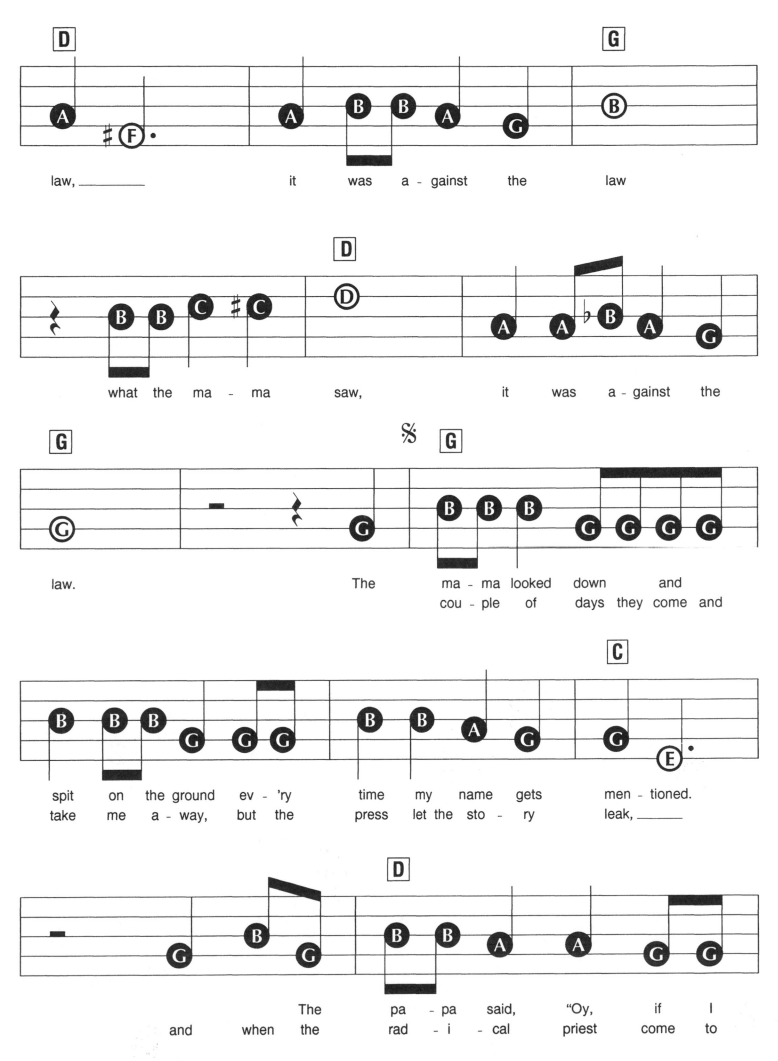

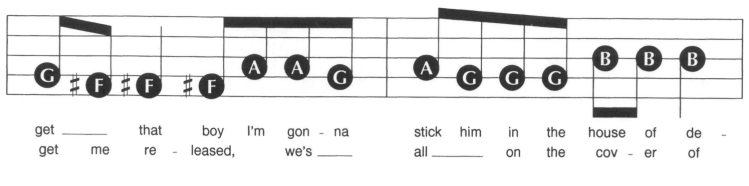

get _____ that boy I'm gon - na stick him in the house of de -
get me re - leased, we's _____ all _____ on the cov - er of

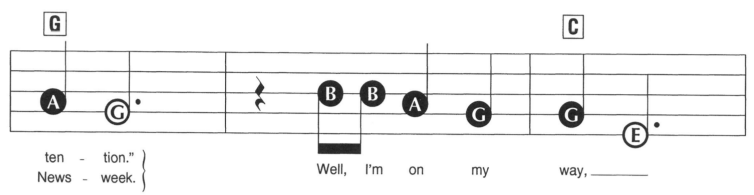

ten - tion."
News - week.

Well, I'm on my way, _____

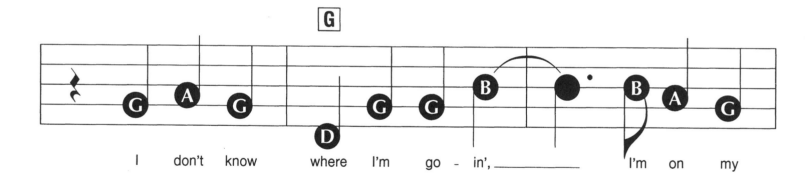

I don't know where I'm go - in', _____ I'm on my

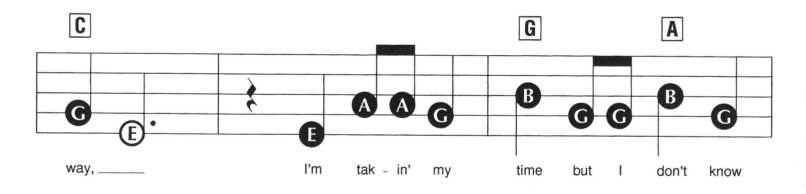

way, _____ I'm tak - in' my time but I don't know

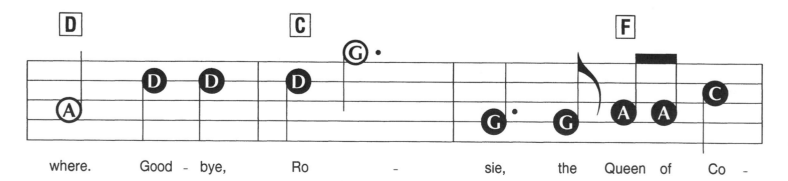

where. Good - bye, Ro - sie, the Queen of Co -

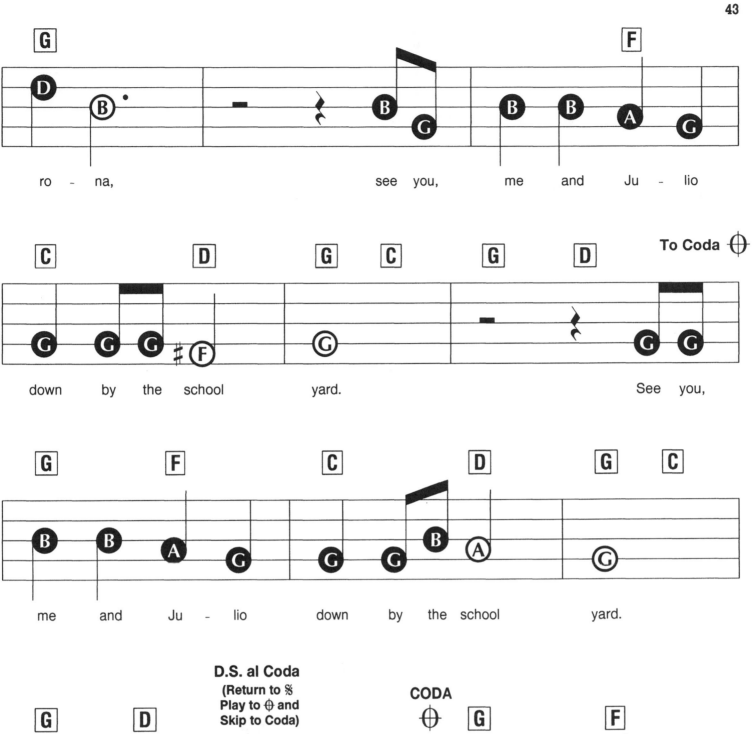

See you,
me and Ju – lio down by the school yard.

To Coda ⊕

See you,

me and Ju – lio down by the school yard.

D.S. al Coda
(Return to ℅
Play to ⊕ and
Skip to Coda)

In a

CODA

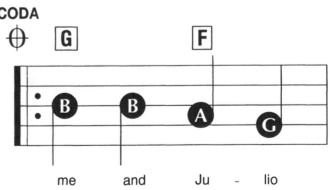

me and Ju – lio

Repeat and Fade

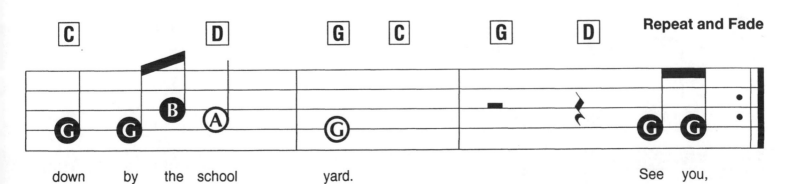

down by the school yard. See you,

Mrs. Robinson

Registration 5
Rhythm: Swing

Words and Music by
Paul Simon

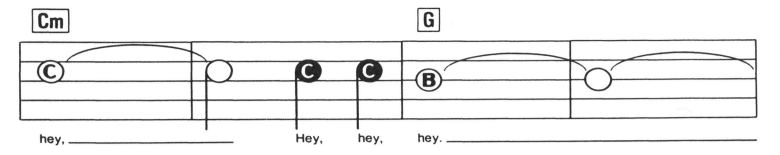

hey, _____ Hey, hey, hey. _____

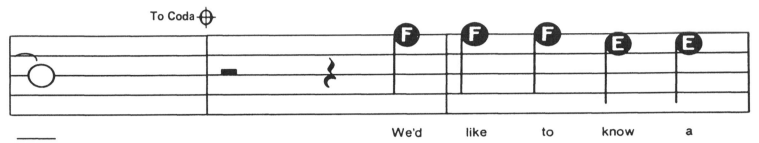

To Coda

G7

_____ We'd like to know a

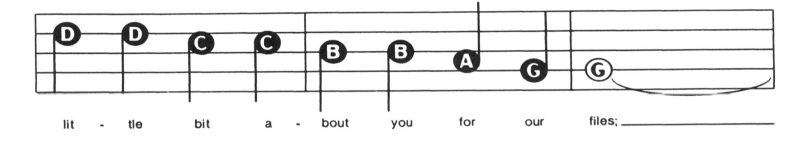

lit - tle bit a - bout you for our files; _____

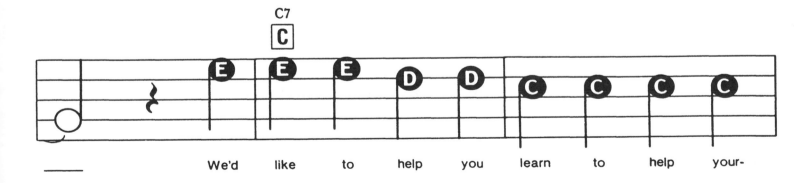

C7
C

_____ We'd like to help you learn to help your-

F7
F

self. _____ Look a - round you,

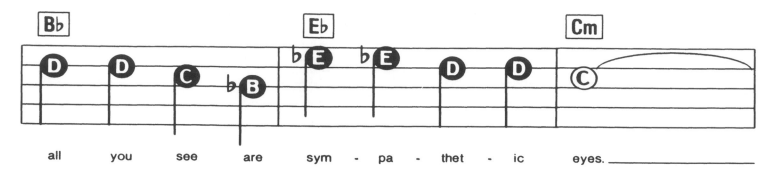

all you see are sym - pa - thet - ic eyes._____

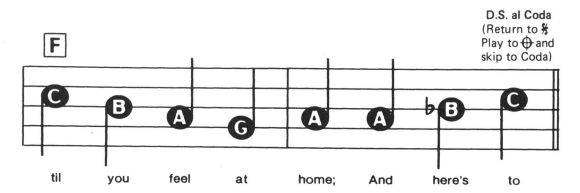

_____ Stroll a - round the grounds un-

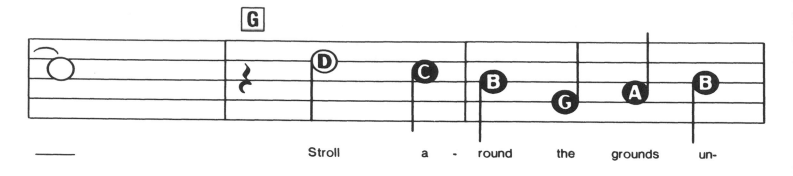

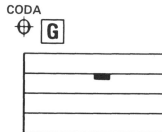

D.S. al Coda
(Return to %
Play to ⊕ and
skip to Coda)

CODA
⊕

til you feel at home; And here's to

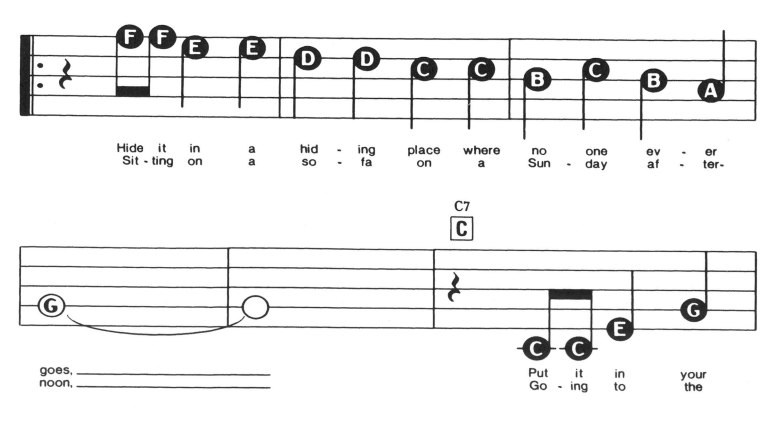

Hide it in a hid - ing place where no one ev - er
Sit - ting on a so - fa on a Sun - day af - ter-

goes,_____
noon,_____

Put it in your
Go - ing to the

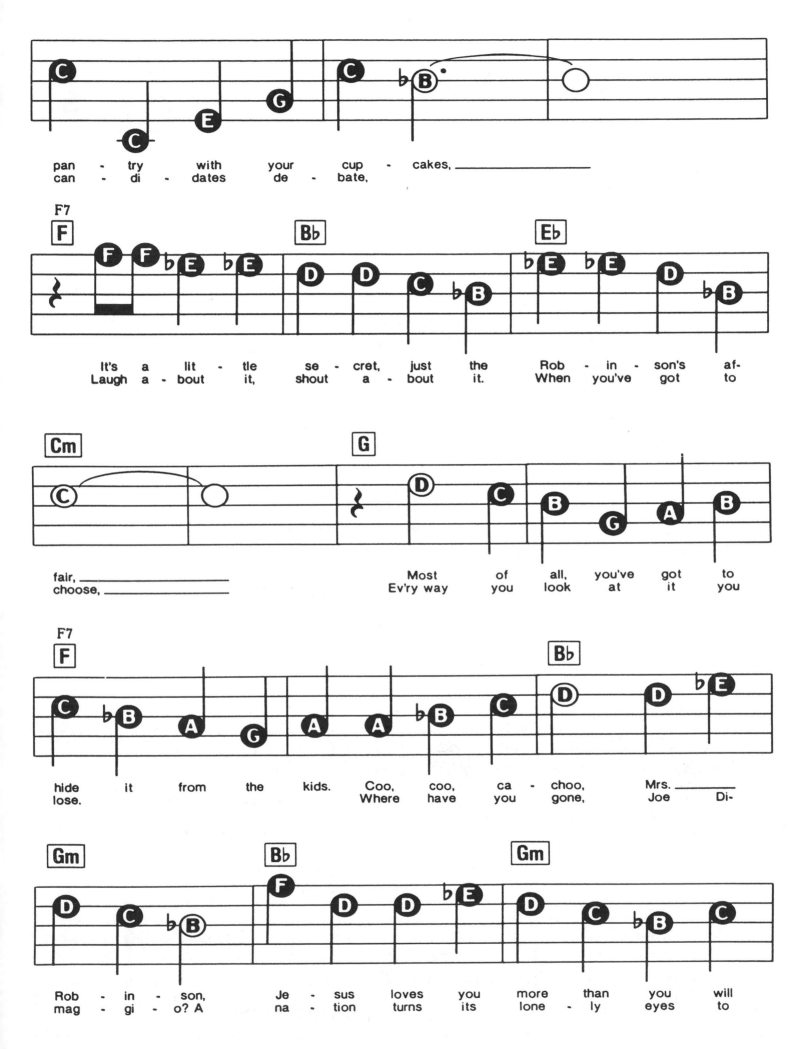

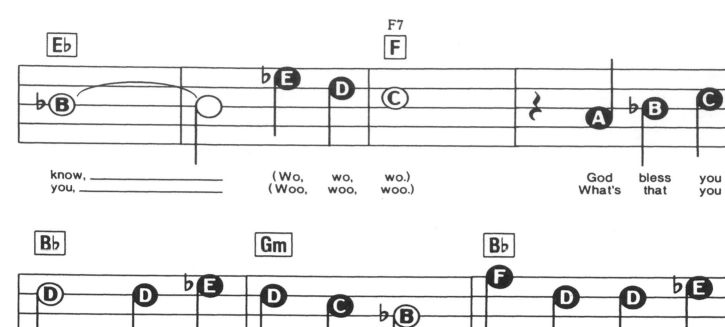

know, _____ (Wo, wo, wo.) God bless you
you, _____ (Woo, woo, woo.) What's that you

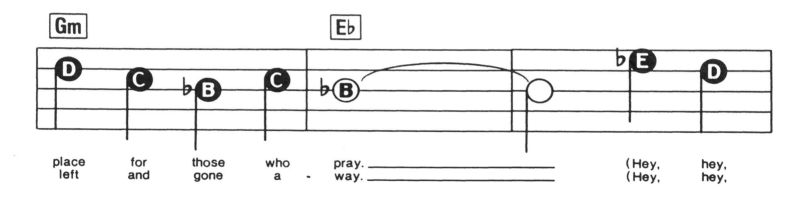

please, Mrs. _____ Rob - in - son, Heav - en holds a
say, Mrs. _____ Rob - in - son, "Jolt - in' Joe" has

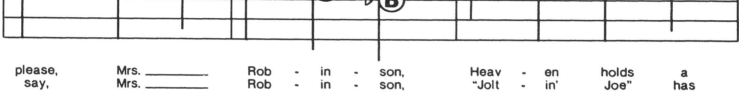

place for those who pray. _____ (Hey, hey,
left and gone a - way. _____ (Hey, hey,

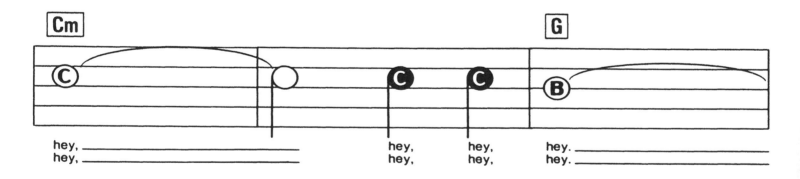

hey, _____ hey, hey, hey. _____
hey, _____ hey, hey, hey. _____

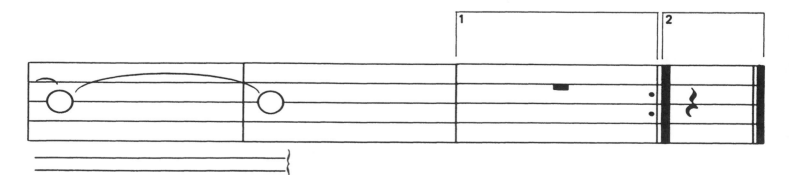

Slip Slidin' Away

Registration 2
Rhythm: Rock

Words and Music by
Paul Simon

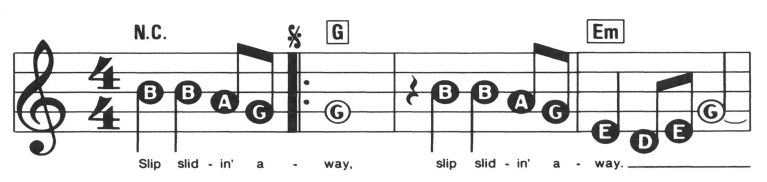

Slip slid - in' a - way,   slip slid - in' a - way. _____

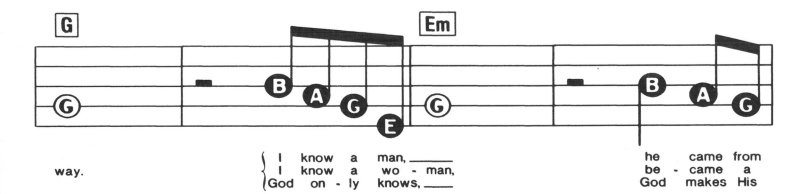

_____ You know the near - er your des - ti - na - tion the more you're slip slid - in' a-

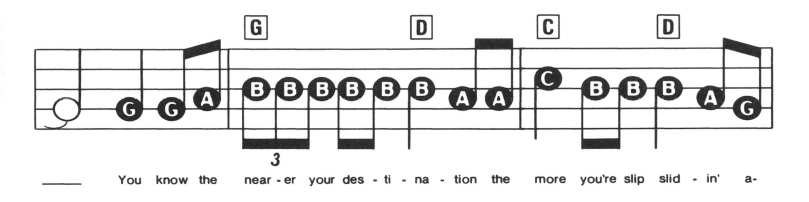

way.   { I know a man, _____   he came from
I know a wo - man,   be - came a
God on - ly knows, _____   God makes His

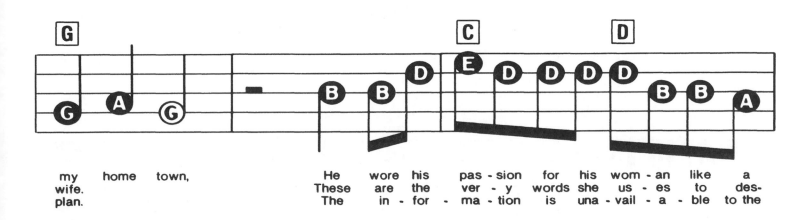

my home town,   He wore his pas - sion for his wom - an like a
wife.   These are the ver - y words she us - es to des-
plan.   The in - for - ma - tion is una - vail - a - ble to the

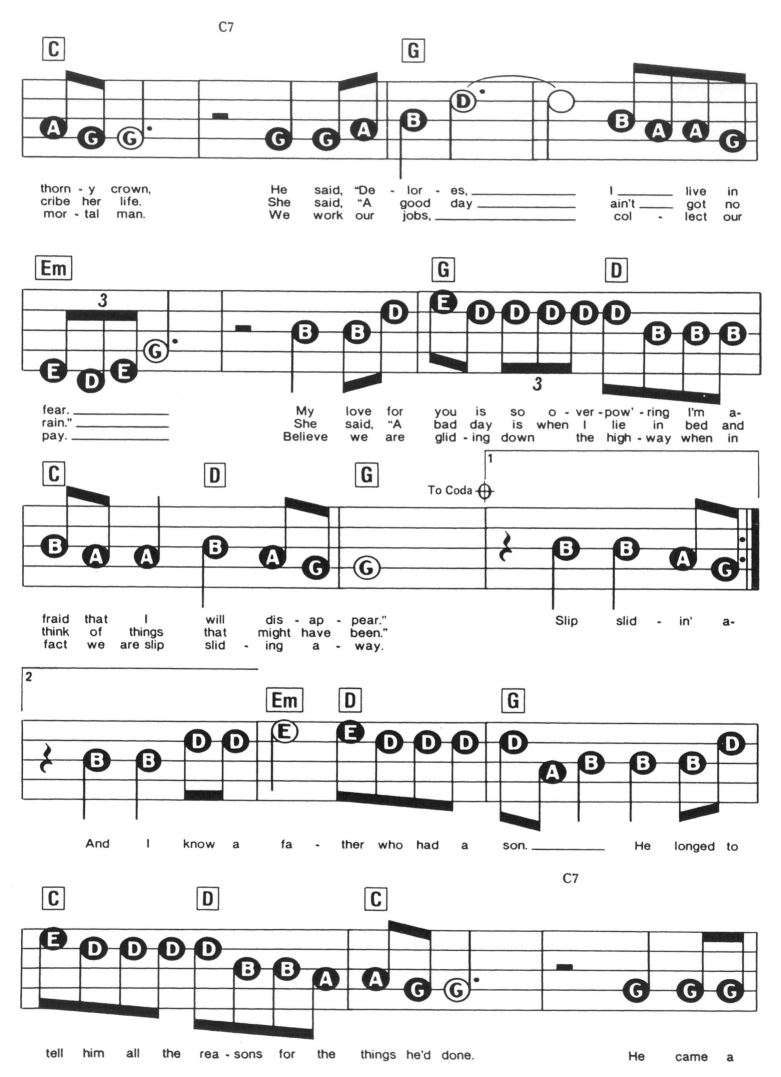

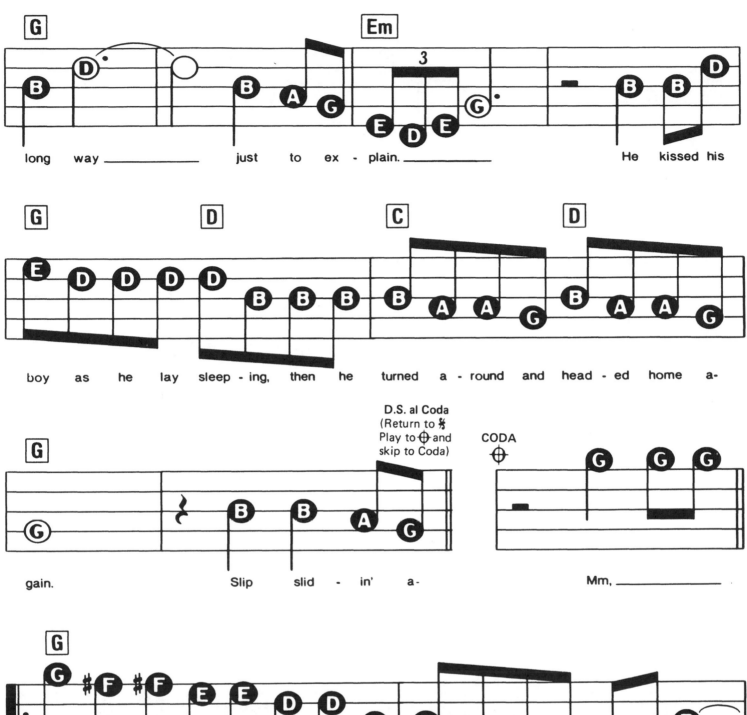

long way _____ just to ex - plain. _____ He kissed his

boy as he lay sleep - ing, then he turned a - round and head - ed home a-

gain. Slip slid - in' a-

D.S. al Coda
(Return to 𝄋
Play to ⨁ and
skip to Coda)

CODA ⨁

Mm, _____

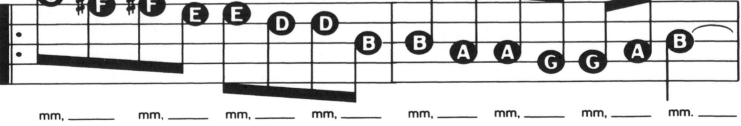

mm, ____ mm, ____ mm, ____ mm, ____ mm, ____ mm, ____ mm, ____ mm.

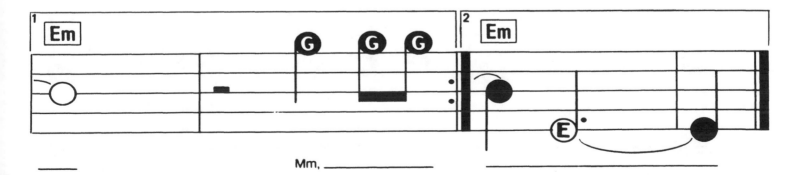

Mm, _____

My Little Town

Registration 1
Rhythm: Slow Rock or Ballad

Words and Music by
Paul Simon

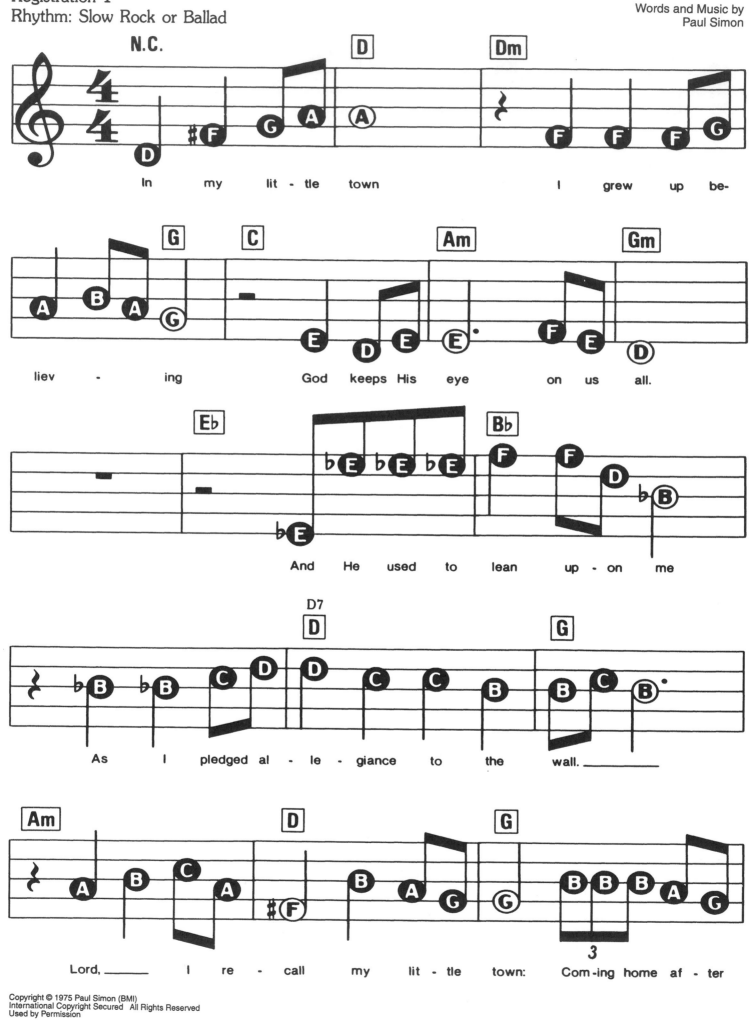

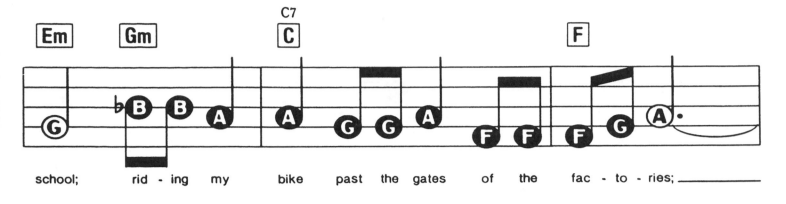

school; rid - ing my bike past the gates of the fac - to - ries; _____

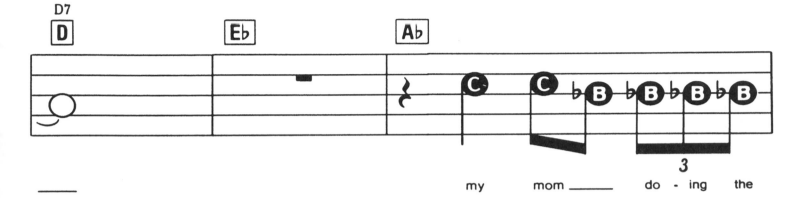

_____ my mom _____ do - ing the

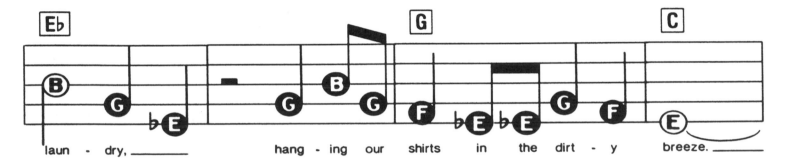

laun - dry, _____ hang - ing our shirts in the dirt - y breeze. _____

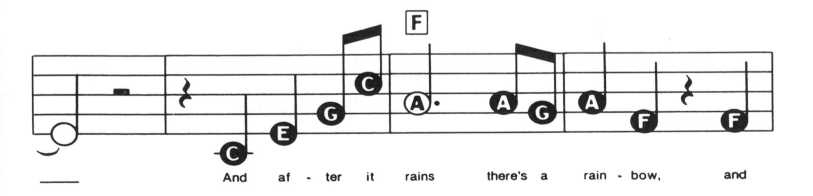

_____ And af - ter it rains there's a rain - bow, and

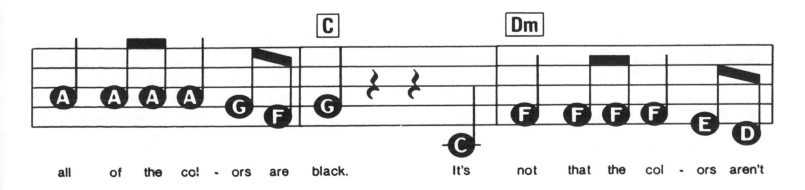

all of the col - ors are black. It's not that the col - ors aren't

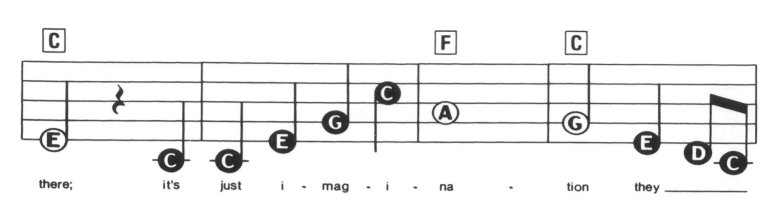

there; it's just i - mag - i - na - tion they _____

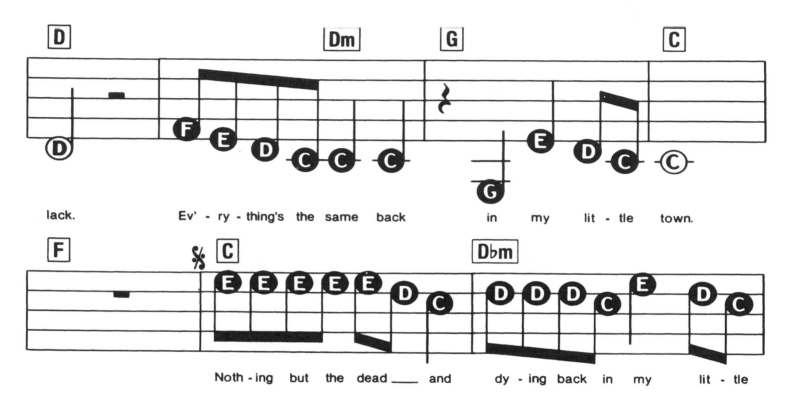

lack. Ev' - ry - thing's the same back in my lit - tle town.

Noth - ing but the dead ____ and dy - ing back in my lit - tle

town, _____ noth - ing but the dead ____ and

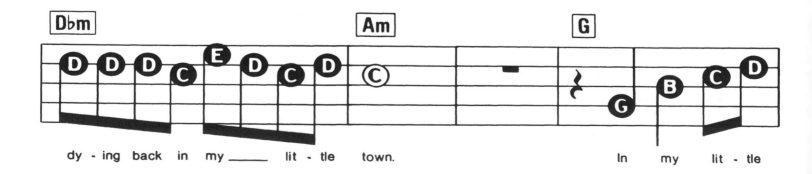

dy - ing back in my ____ lit - tle town. In my lit - tle

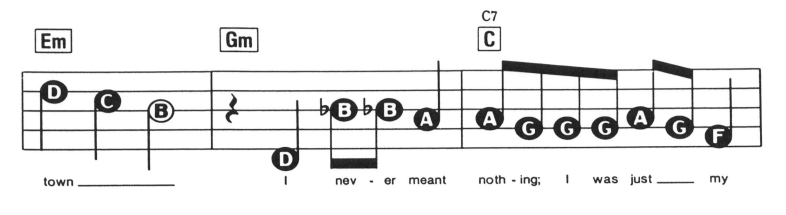

town _____ I nev - er meant noth - ing; I was just _____ my

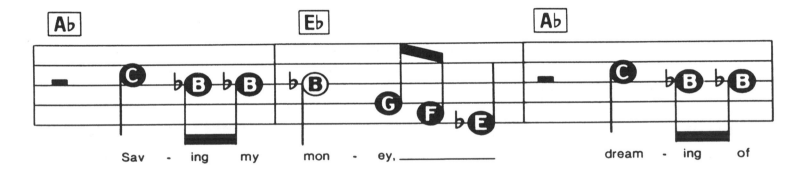

fa - ther's son, mm. _____

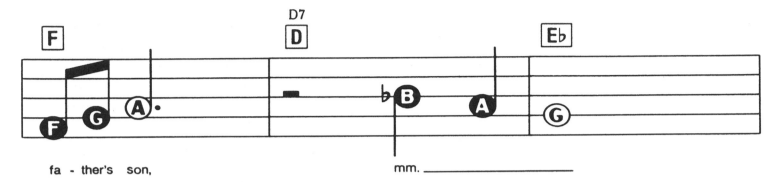

Sav - ing my mon - ey, _____ dream - ing of

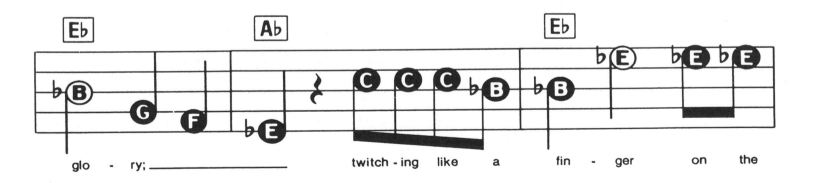

glo - ry; _____ twitch - ing like a fin - ger on the

D.S. and Fade
(Return to 𝄋 and Fade)

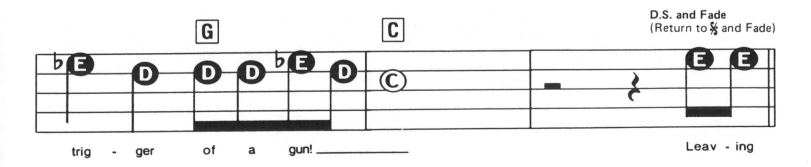

trig - ger of a gun! _____ Leav - ing

Scarborough Fair

Registration 3
Rhythm: Waltz

Arrangement and original counter melody by Paul Simon
and Arthur Garfunkel

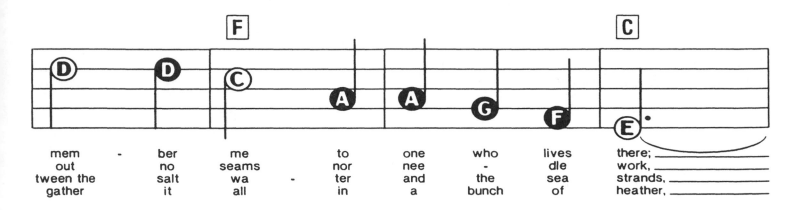

mem - ber   me   to   one   who   lives   there;
out   no   seams   nor   nee - dle   work,
tween the   salt   it   wa - ter   and   the   sea   strands,
gather   it   all   in   a   bunch   of   heather,

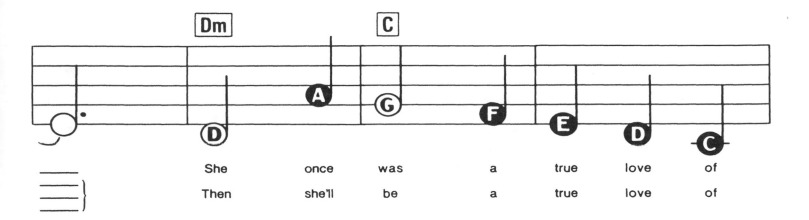

She   once   was   a   true   love   of
Then   she'll   be   a   true   love   of

1,2,3

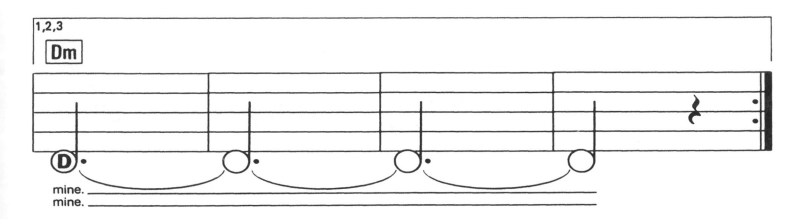

mine.
mine.

4

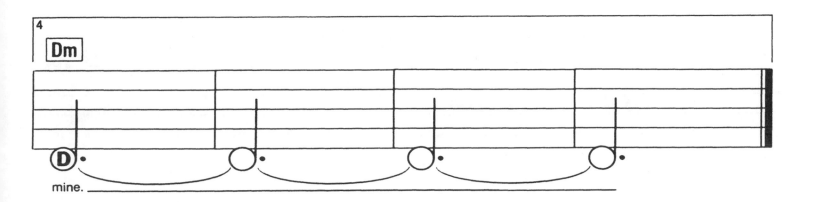

mine.

The Sound of Silence

Registration 1
Rhythm: Slow Rock or Ballad

Words and Music by
Paul Simon

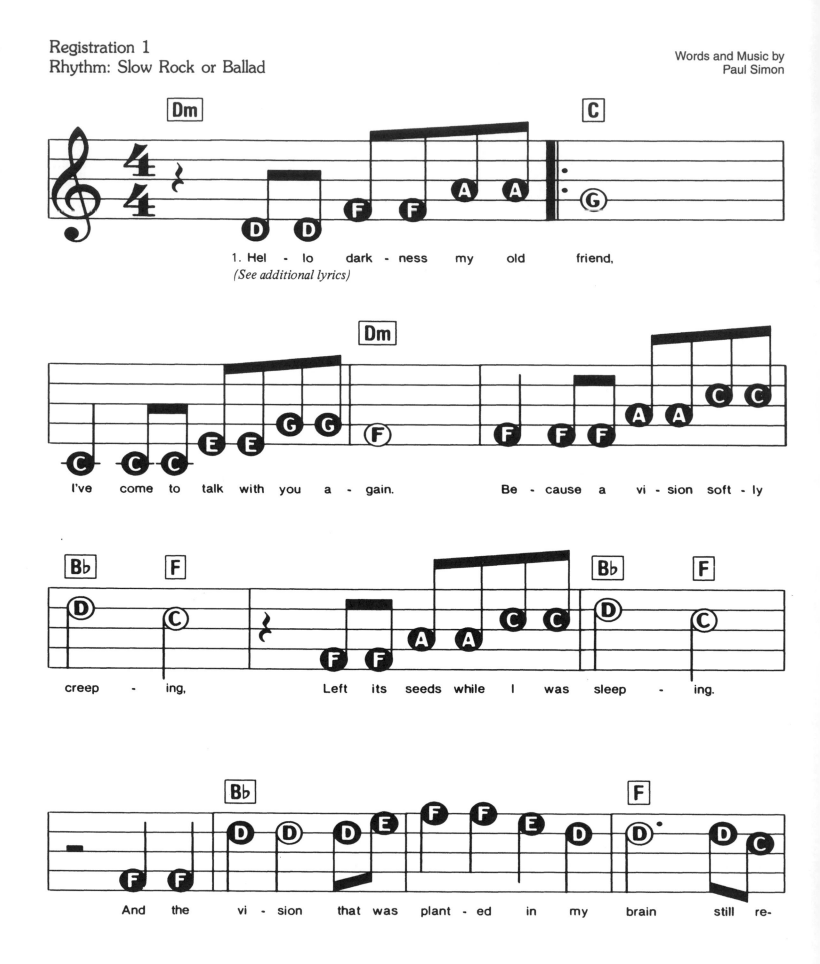

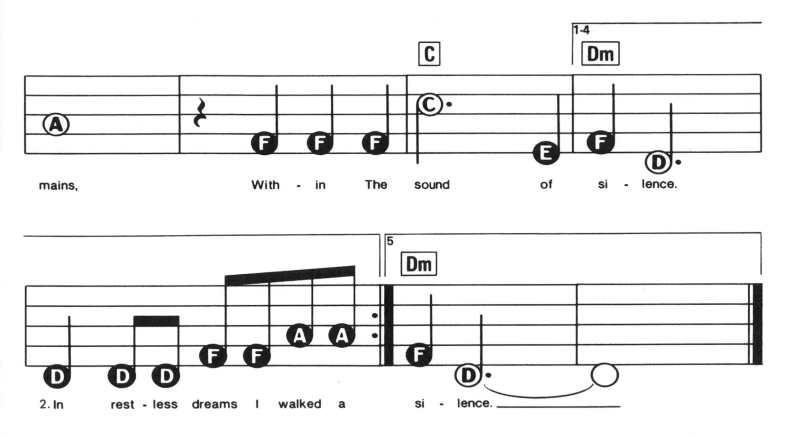

2. In restless dreams I walked alone
   Narrow streets of cobblestone,
   'Neath the halo of a street lamp,
   I turned my collar to the cold and damp
   When my eyes were stabbed by the flash of a neon light
   That split the night and touched the sound of silence.

3. And in the naked light I saw
   Ten thousand people, maybe more.
   People talking without speaking,
   People hearing without listening,
   People writing songs that voices never share
   And no one dare disturb the sound of silence.

4. "Fools!" said I, "You do not know
   Silence like a cancer grows.
   Hear my words that I might teach you,
   Take my arms that I might reach you."
   But my words like silent raindrops fell,
   And echoed in the wells of silence.

5. And the people bowed and prayed
   To the neon god they made.
   And the sign flashed out its warning.
   In the words that it was forming,
   And the signs said "the words of the prophets
   Are written on the subway walls and tenement halls."
   And whispered in the sounds of silence.

Still Crazy After All These Years

Registration 1
Rhythm: Waltz

Words and Music by
Paul Simon

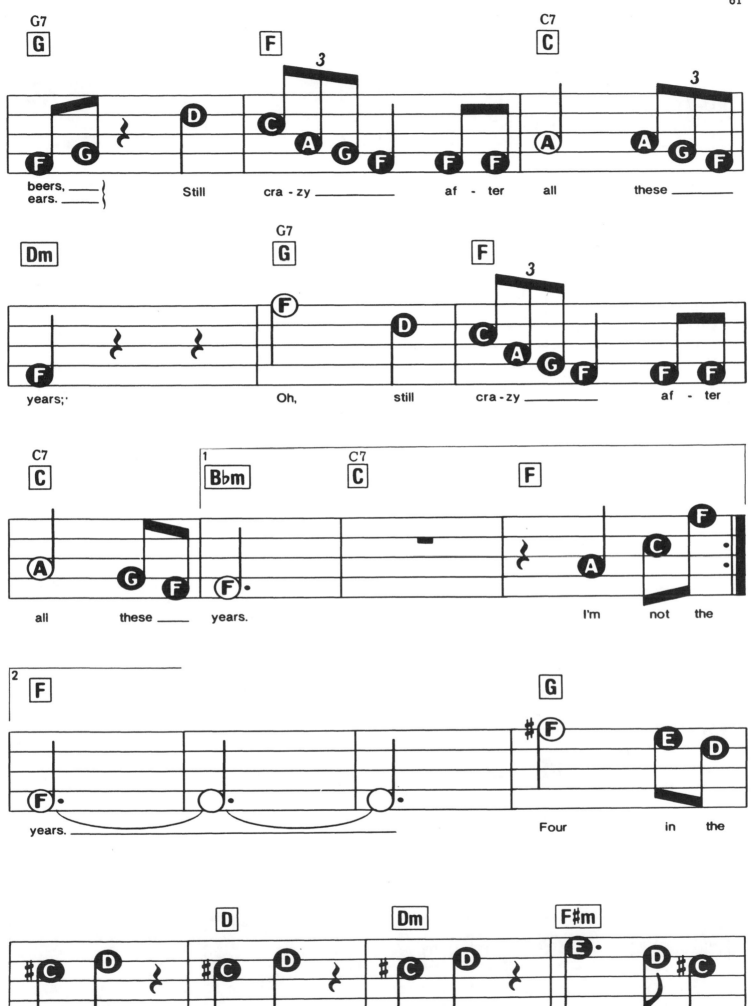

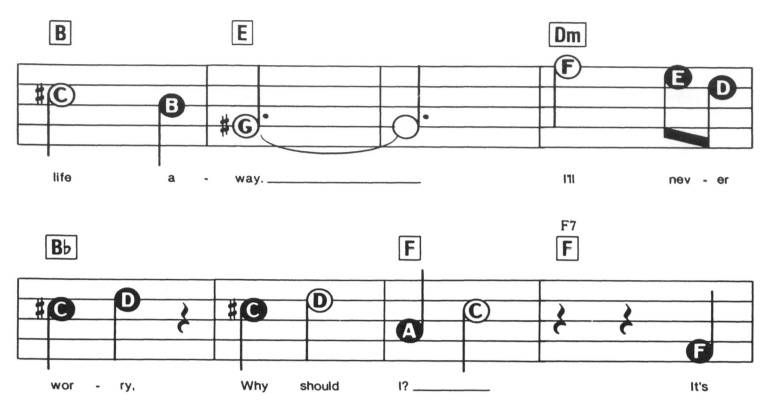

life a - way. _____ I'll nev - er

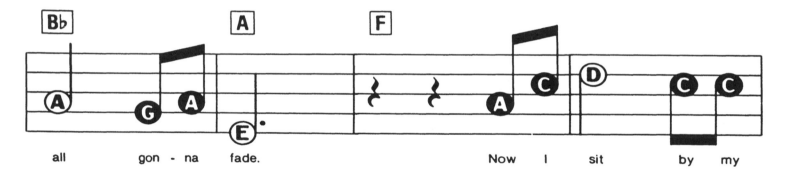

wor - ry, Why should I? _____ It's

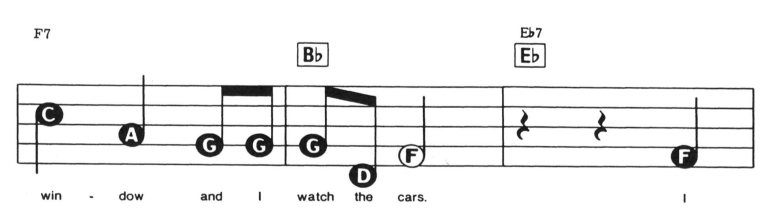

all gon - na fade. Now I sit by my

win - dow and I watch the cars. I

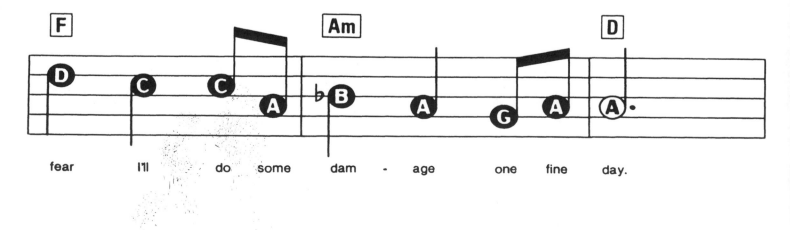

fear I'll do some dam - age one fine day.

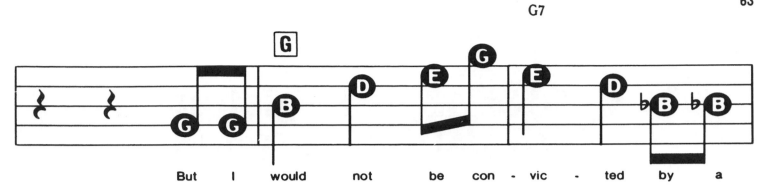

But I would not be con - vic - ted by a

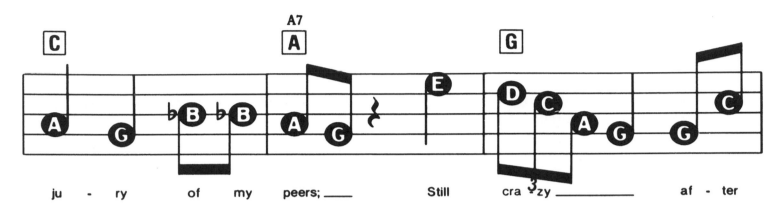

ju - ry of my peers; ____ Still cra - zy ____ af - ter

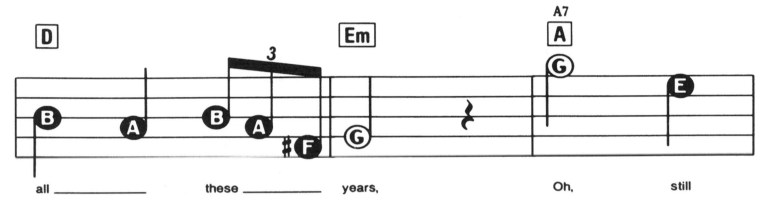

all ____ these ____ years, Oh, still

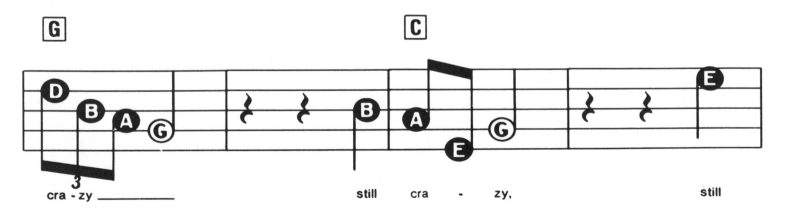

cra - zy ____ still cra - zy, still

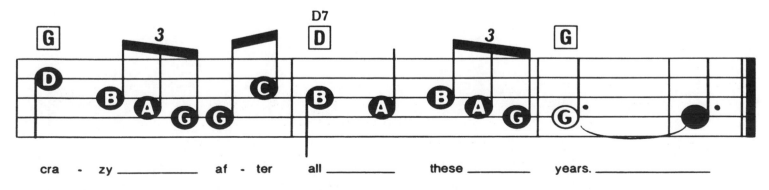

cra - zy ____ af - ter all ____ these ____ years. ____

Registration Guide

- Match the Registration number on the song to the corresponding numbered category below. Select and activate an Instrumental sound available on your instrument.

- Choose an automatic rhythm appropriate to the mood and style of the song. (Consult your Owner's Guide for proper operation of automatic rhythm features.)

- Adjust the tempo and volume controls to comfortable settings.

Registration

1	Mellow	Flutes, Clarinet, Oboe, Flugel Horn, Trombone, French Horn, Organ Flutes
2	Ensemble	Brass Section, Sax Section, Wind Ensemble, Full Organ, Theater Organ
3	Strings	Violin, Viola, Cello, Fiddle, String Ensemble, Pizzicato, Organ Strings
4	Guitars	Acoustic/Electric Guitars, Banjo, Mandolin, Dulcimer, Ukulele, Hawaiian Guitar
5	Mallets	Vibraphone, Marimba, Xylophone, Steel Drums, Bells, Celesta, Chimes
6	Liturgical	Pipe Organ, Hand Bells, Vocal Ensemble, Choir, Organ Flutes
7	Bright	Saxophones, Trumpet, Mute Trumpet, Synth Leads, Jazz/Gospel Organs
8	Piano	Piano, Electric Piano, Honky Tonk Piano, Harpsichord, Clavi
9	Novelty	Melodic Percussion, Wah Trumpet, Synth, Whistle, Kazoo, Perc. Organ
10	Bellows	Accordion, French Accordion, Mussette, Harmonica, Pump Organ, Bagpipes